A Dumbarton Childhood

Joseph Mcloughlin

Acknowledgements

With grateful thanks to my big sister Marie Therese Briglin for her invaluable help and who also contributed with some childhood stories which had faded from my memory over the years.

Thanks to my old school friend Murt O'Connell for his help in recalling some distant school memories and to my cousin Jim Gow who proof-read the manuscript with his "fresh eyes."

Thanks to the internet Facebook pages where I posted requests for information and of course received an abundance of answers from the beautiful people of Dumbarton:-

Dumbarton Memories.

Overtoun Babies.

The Great Brucehill Story.

Dumbarton families Old and New.

St Patrick's High School Former Pupils.

Dedications

To my beautiful wife Gracia Patricia Ureña Espa for her motivation, patience and encouragement and for inspiring me to tell these stories.

To my children so that they may have a clearer understanding of my childhood and teenage years and of course my love of Dumbarton, Scotland.

To the memory of my parents Owen and May Mcloughlin (nee Gow).

To Sons and Daughters of the Rock wherever they may be in the world.

About the author

Joseph Mcloughlin

A true Son of the Rock

Born in Overtoun Maternity Home in Dumbarton, Scotland on 24th December 1951.My first childhood home was 13, Clyde Street.

My mum was May Mcloughlin (nee Gow) and my dad Owen Mcloughlin, my older sister Marie Therese Briglin (nee Mcloughlin) is 3 years older than me.

We lived in 6e, Carrick Terrace, Castlehill before moving to 30, Caledonia Terrace, Brucehill when I was 8 years old then 44, Glencairn Road.

I attended West Bridgend Primary and Saint Patrick's High schools.

I lived in Dumbarton until 1972 when I moved to Hull, England.

In 1976 I moved again to Bristol.

I studied English for a degree at the Open University and passed with honours and became an English Teacher with the British Council, an organisation which provides an English education to underprivileged children..

I came to Spain as an English teacher in 2005 and taught English in Madrid before moving to Caravaca de la Cruz, a beautiful small city in the south of Spain. I met and fell in love with my beautiful, Spanish wife and we married in Bali, Indonesia in 2013.

I opened my own Language School in 2009 where I now work as an English Teacher. I took up writing along with my other hobbies of painting, photography, reading and walking and cycling in the beautiful surrounding mountains of Southern Spain.

I had often considered writing my autobiography but never thought that my stories would be interesting enough for other people, apart from my close family to read.

So with encouragement of my wife I decided to write my memoirs about my childhood in the town I still call my home... Dumbarton, Scotland.

In 2016, after three years and many hours of blood, sweat, tears and strong Spanish coffee, my autobiography "A Dumbarton Childhood" was born.

For more information and to see photographs relating to these memoirs:-

Website:-

http://jomac65.wix.com/author

Facebook page:-

www.facebook.com/A Dumbarton Childhood

I MISS THE LOCHS, I MISS THE GLENS

I MISS THE HEATHER, I MISS THE FERNS

I MISS THE STREAMS WITH THE WEE STONE BRIDGES

I MISS BEING EATEN ALIVE BY MIDGES.

I MISS DUMBARTON, I MISS THE CLYDE

SHIPS SAILING BY ON THE EVENING TIDE

I MISS GLASGOW ON A SATURDAY NIGHT,

I MISS BEING ASKED IF I WANT A FIGHT

I MISS GOING DANCING "UP THE TOON"

I MISS THE STEAMER TRIPS TO DUNOON

I MISS THE WEATHER, I MISS THE WAY

YOU GET 4 DIFFERENT SEASONS ON THE SAME DAY

I MISS THE PEOPLE AND THE GLESGA PATTER

I MISS THE BARRAS AND THE FRIENDLY CHATTER

I MISS THE PUBS AND THE WEE HARD MEN

I MISS THE WAY THEY CALL ME "BIG YIN"

I MISS BEING ASKED IF I FANCY A BEVVY

I MISS A WEE HAUF AN A PINT O HEAVY

I MISS BURNS NIGHT AND HOGMANAY

THE SKIRL O THE PIPES AND A JIG BEING PLAYED

I MISS GOING TO PARTIES WITH A "CARRY OOT"

SINGING FLOWER O SCOTLAND WHILE TAPPING MY FOOT

I MISS HIGHLAND TOFFEE AND MACAROON BARS

I MISS CANDY BALLS KEPT IN JARS

I MISS SQUARE SAUSAGE, HAGGIS AND NEEPS

WALKING HOME EATING BLACK PUDDING AND CHIPS

I COULD CARRY ON LISTING THE THINGS THAT I MISS

BUT THE LONGER I'M GONE THE LONGER THE LIST

I'M HOMESICK FOR DUMBARTON, THERE ISN'T A CURE

BUT ONE THING'S FOR CERTAIN, ONE THING'S FOR SURE

YOU CAN TAKE THE MAN OUT OF DUMBARTON

BUT NOBODY CAN.......

TAKE DUMBARTON OUT OF THE MAN

Table of Contents

Introduction

It's hot and sunny as usual, probably around 25 degrees but here, sitting on my balcony in Southern Spain overlooking the fertile valleys of fruit orchards and vineyards in the afternoon sun it feels much hotter.

This is November, the autumn, but here in Caravaca de la Cruz where I live the good life, the sun burns down on us for an average 320 days a year and we are truly blessed with clean, fresh air and a wonderful, healthy climate.

This small, typically Spanish, historic town in the mountains of Murcia is where I now live. I have been living here since 2006 when I arrived here from Madrid to teach English in a local school. I now have my own private language school, I am married to my beautiful Spanish wife Garcia Patricia Ureña Espa and have absorbed and integrated into the typical Spanish lifestyle of fiestas, siestas, eating paella outside all year and drinking fine wines and cold beer from a glass straight out of the freezer.

My varied, interesting and adventurous journey through life before settling here in Spain is a long story, for another time, which I´m sure will form chapters of a future book.

I sit here in quiet reflection most days having lunch, reading, listening to music and relaxing before returning to school for afternoon classes. This is my private time when my mind is free to travel and it takes full advantage, sifting out all interference and meandering through my past.......

Dumbarton, the town of my childhood. My various family homes...13, Clyde Street,

6e Carrick Terrace, Castlehill,...30,Caledonia Terrace,...44,Glencairn Road ,Brucehill,.

Denny's shipyard, Dumbarton Castle, Ballantine's Distillery, Levengrove Park, St Patrick's High School, Castlehill, Brucehill, Westcliff, Bellsmyre. So many varied and happy memories of a life gone by so many years ago.

Going to the minor's pictures on a Saturday morning dressed as a cowboy, then buying chips from Tony Biaggi's chip shop with lots of salt and vinegar and eating them out of a newspaper dripping vinegar through my fingers, later to be licked clean, while walking home.

Saturday nights spent dancing in the Burgh Hall. Having a wee fly drink of Eldorado "Doon the Quay" before going in for Dutch courage to ask the girls to dance, or if you were lucky a snog and a lumber or even a wee "feelie"...these are memories etched forever in my memory.

Riding our bikes and being chased by the Parkie in Levengrove Park, playing Sunday football 20 a side in the Posties Park, families having picnics "Doon the Shore" on the rare, hot, sunny, summer days. Days out to Helensburgh or Loch Lomond, sailing on the steamers "Doon the Water "to Dunoon and Rothsay

These are the nostalgic, precious memories of a long ago, interesting and varied life in Dumbarton.

My daydreams are interrupted by my wife.........

"Are you O.K. darling?"..... She asks me in her beautiful Spanish accent...

"Do you want anything?"

"Yes please baby..... A nice cold gin and tonic with ice would be fantastic please."

The sun burns relentlessly down on the valley below, the trees are starting to turn beautiful shades of brown, orange, yellow, and red. The scent of jasmine mixed with lemons and oranges hangs heavy in the air whilst a semi-transparent heat haze envelopes the distant mountains.

The fruit trees have all been harvested and the valley is preparing for what we laughingly call winter.

Two months of cooler weather lies ahead, we are thankful that the shadows are lengthening and the long, sweltering, oppressively hot summer days are now behind us and we can feel the cooler fresher air moving gently across the valley again and hoping it brings some much needed rain to replenish the dried up Rivers Argos and Segura.

The Holy City of Caravaca is a traditional Spanish town of 25.000 people nestling in the fertile foothills of the Sierra Espuña and Revolcadores mountains, green and lush in winter and burned brown in the summer. The long, sandy, tourist beaches of the south coast are just over an hour away.

The beautiful, historic Spanish cities of Madrid, Granada, Seville, Valencia, Cordoba, Toledo and Cadiz are all an easy drive from here...

This is now my life, my home where I live and have settled.....but my heart will always be in Dumbarton, my hometown where I was born and grew up, the town which shaped me into the person I am today, and armed me with the knowledge and experience which have served me so well throughout my life.

I am who I am today because of the childhood and teenage experiences I had while growing up in Dumbarton....I am proud to be a true "Son of the Rock"

I move my chair further into the shade to protect me from the blaring sun and take another long, slow sip of my gin and tonic, enjoying the cool refreshing taste and listening to the chink of the ice cubes in the glass, while in the clear, blue, cloudless sky a lone eagle circles, majestically overhead.

My mind floods with the memories of my childhood.

Stories which I recount regularly to my Spanish wife, she loves listening to them, they are incredible, funny, tragic, sad, nostalgic but unbelievably they are all true. But how can anyone who hasn't experienced a Scottish 1950's and 60's childhood understand these stories? She knows how important my hometown is to me and how much I miss it.

We visited Dumbarton two years ago because I wanted her to get some idea of the town where I grew up. We walked along the once bustling High Street, now deserted, with empty, boarded up shops…. she wasn't impressed. We climbed up the monolithic castle with its stunning views over the Firth of Clyde which has stood, like a sentinel for centuries as the unmistakable, historic symbol of Dumbarton.

We walked around Levengrove Park, still unchanged over the years, along the shores of the River Clyde where we as children played and families picnicked on summer Sundays. I explained that everything has changed and that the Dumbarton of today isn't the same as when I was a child.

Some things change ….and some things stay the same.

"You should write about your life" she says

"You should share your stories with other people."

I take another long cool sip of my drink…..

"You're absolutely right darling…I will someday."

"Why someday?" she says.

"You should do it now!"

So I did.

Here it is………….

Made in Dumbarton

Monday the 24th of December 1951 was a bitterly cold, dark, winter night. The light of the full moon in the clear, cloudless sky made the crystallized snow glisten and sparkle like a million stars. After several days of snow and sub-zero temperatures the snow on the ground was frozen solid, the bushes crisp and white with frost. The wind whistling gently through the trees made the leaves move, dislodging small drops of frosted snow which floated silently down to settle on the frozen ground surrounding Overtoun House nursing home, Dumbarton, Scotland.

Inside the hospital were a handful of women preparing to give birth, all hoping that their child would be born on Christmas day, the holiest of days, which of course would surely be a special blessing from god.

Overtoun House in the grounds of Overtoun Farm, with stunning views from its hill top location over the River Clyde and Dumbarton, was a beautiful historic old building, constructed in the1860's it was used as a family home for rich doctors and gentry for almost a century, and now, after extensive refurbishment it was put to use as a residential nursing home and maternity unit.

It was 9.45 pm and all the families in their homes in Dumbarton were preparing for Christmas Day and the imminent arrival of Santa Clause whilst trying to calm their over-excited children and put them to bed with threats that if they didn't go to sleep straight away then Father Christmas wouldn't visit and leave them presents. But it was just too exciting for them to sleep with the heady prospect of their stockings being filled with an orange wrapped in tin foil, some nuts and joy of joys perhaps even if they were really lucky, a bar of Fry's Five Boys chocolate.

This bar of chocolate would later be eaten slowly so as to savour the flavour and lengthen the rare special moment of heavenly pleasure, with the melted chocolate being licked and sucked from sticky fingers and then the remains wrapped in silver foil to be hidden and saved to be opened and secretly enjoyed again another day. These were the simple Christmas treats that any child of the 50s appreciated, not for them the demands and high expectations of materialistic future generations, of X- Boxes, Play Stations, computer games and mobile phones.

These were the days when children played outside, not online, their mums called their names, not their mobile phones and if they didn't like what their mum had cooked......then they didn't eat.

This was Christmas 1951 and families were still recovering from the post war austerity rationing measures imposed by the government. They had experienced food and clothes rationing and their level of expectations were limited. The children would wake up early while the frost was still sticking to the inside of the bedroom windows, stick their head out from under the blankets and mountain of heavy overcoats which had been put on top of them by their parents in an effort to keep them warm, and would watch their breath condensate and float across the room.

Some would pretend it was smoke from an invisible cigarette, tentatively thrust a foot still with a thick woollen sock on it out into the freezing air, then launch themselves out of bed onto an ice cold linoleum covered floor and run to the kitchen, which was warmed by the gas cooker to see if father Christmas had drunk the glass of whisky and eaten the slice of shortbread which they had left out for him the night before.

Meantime May Mcloughlin nee Gow was in the late stages of her long labour.

This was May's second pregnancy. She had given birth to a daughter, her first child three years before. Marie Therese was now 3 years old and excited about the imminent arrival of her special Christmas present from Santa Clause, a wee brother or sister. A sister would be her preferred sibling, but, no matter if it was a boy she could still play babies with him and dress him up in her favourite doll clothes and take him for walks in her wee toy pram.

May's husband, Owen a hole borer in Denny's shipyard was at home waiting for any news. In those days husbands weren't welcome or expected at the birth of their children. They were barely tolerated at visiting times but absolutely forbidden to attend the birth. This was woman's' work the man had done his macho bit nine months before and remained resolutely detached from the whole process until the baby popped out......

"How's the wife Owen?'

"Aye fine.

"Had the baby yet?"

"No....Don't think so"

"Another pint a heavy?"

"Aye sure"

"Here Owen huv a wee whisky as well... Sure ye must be worn out with all this waiting."

The labour pains were now coming rapidly when nurses wheeled May into the delivery room. As the big clock struck ten it was obvious that it was only a matter of minutes now. The midwife joked that May should cross her legs and try to hold on for a couple of hours until after midnight when it would then be Christmas day and her child would be the first baby born on this holiest of days, Jesus's birthday, surely a great honour and privilege. But it was time, there was no holding back the process of birth, nature had decided that this baby was fully baked and oven ready.

I was about to enter the world regardless of date or time....

10.10pm...push....breathe...push...Breathe......

10.12pm... push...push ....The head...

10.14pm....push.....push.... The shoulders...

10.15pm.... big push....Plop!!

Here I was, a little blotchy bundle of snot and slime. I had arrived in the world head first.

Grabbed by the ankles and hung upside down by the midwife, a quick blow up my nose and mouth to clear the mucus and a hefty slap on the bare arse and with a first deep breath and a loud scream I let the world know that I was alive and healthy and with a good strong pair of lungs.

"It`s a wee boy May" announced the midwife.

Holding me up with hands and legs flailing around, I was wrapped in a towel and introduced to my mum.

"May and Owen Mcloughlin are happy to announce the arrival of a son Joseph.

6lb 4oz. Born on Monday 24th December 1951 at 10.15pm in Overtoun House Nursing home Dumbarton. Grateful thanks to the nursing staff. "Deo Gracias."

Said the notice in the births section of that week's Lennox Herald.

In his Christmas day speech to the nation the following day King George 6th failed to mention the momentous, earth shattering event which had taken place in a small town in Scotland just the night before.

After the regulatory three or four days in hospital for rest and recovery May finally left Overtoun House with her wee bundle of joy and headed home to 13,Clyde Street.

Clyde Street was where we lived. A long street which stretched from Glasgow Road to Dumbarton Castle, passing the gates of Denny's Shipyard. This was social housing for the workers of the shipyard and provided at low rent to the employees of the yard.

The houses were small and all joined together in a terrace, with closes which opened out onto back yards where there were the communal wash houses and of course the outside toilets.

So here I was wearing my wee blue knitted hat and jumper in my big Pedigree pram being shown off around the streets of Dumbarton by my proud mum and everyone putting the traditional silver sixpence in the pram for luck.

"Ach sure whit a bonnie wee baby May."

"Whit's his name?"

"Joseph...He was born on Christmas eve."

"Ahh whit a great wee Christmas present."

"He's got his dad's eyes"

"Aye....Wan on the pot an the other up the chimney"

So here I was, born into a place and time in history.

Dumbarton, a historic town 14 miles north west of Glasgow and only 8 miles from Balloch and the mouth of Loch Lomond. The ancient capital of Strathclyde it's a town with a close-knit community of around 25,000 people. The majority of adults worked in either Denny's shipyard or Ballantine's whisky distillery.

The outstanding feature of the town is the castle which is situated at the point where the River Clyde meets the River Leven and here, more or less unchanged since time began the ancient lump of volcanic rock fortress known as Dumbarton Castle rises out of the river like a phoenix and overlooks the town. Next to the castle was Denny's shipyard where the majority of the towns male population worked and around the shipyard were the streets of small terraced houses built in the early 1900's and where the shipyard workers lived. These houses were very basic and consisted of one bedroom and a living room which also included the open fire which doubled as the kitchen. The toilet was outside and shared with 3 or 4 other families.

Our house at no 13 had been my Grannie Gow's house until, because of overcrowding, she was moved to the new council house scheme in Brucehill.

My grannie Gow had brought up her family in this tiny house, a family which consisted of nine children. My grannie and all the girls slept in one room in two beds and my granddad and all the boys slept in the living room which had a set-in bed and a Hurley bed, so called because it hurled away during the day to be hidden under the big bed and was always complete with pillows and blankets. When asked how they managed to have nine children in these conditions my grannie always said that my granddad had to come into her room late at night to wind up the clock, now whether that was some kind of euphemism for procreation I don't know.

So my grannie moved to lovely, big, new council house at 17, Caledonia Terrace, Brucehill, where she had four bedrooms, a living room, kitchen and the luxury of an inside bathroom with a bath, and an enormous garden where vegetables such as potatoes, carrots and cabbages were grown, although I'm sure that my granddad continued with his ritual of winding up the clock.

This was the 1950s. Families were settling in to the post war lifestyle. After years of poverty and rationing during the war things were now improving and the future was looking rosier. Britain had a new prime minister the newly re-elected Winston Churchill and a new monarch. After the death of King George 6th in February 1952 his daughter the young Queen Elizabeth 2nd took the throne, so there was a feeling of optimism in the air.

My father had a good job in Denny's shipyard in the engine shop as a hole borer I think that meant that wherever they needed a hole to put in a screw or bolt my dad came along with his drill and made one, he always said he was the most important person in the yard because without him the ship couldn't be built, but, to be fair, I think that all the other tradesmen thought the same about their jobs too. As was tradition my mum was a housewife, looking after the home, doing the cooking, cleaning and bringing up the children, me and my sister. This was a time when it was unusual for a woman to work, the majority leaving school and getting married early. Children normally came along quickly too.

So my early life was a cosy little room and kitchen house in Clyde Street, the houses were old,damp and in desperate need of repair, the toilets were outside in the back yard and as many families lived in such close proximity to one another and as all the men worked together in Denny's shipyard there was a family atmosphere where everyone knew each other, so if my mum needed to pop out to the shops she could just ask a neighbour to keep an eye on us for a while until she came back.

It was during one of these shopping trips that I made my first bid for freedom....

I was only three years old, but already blessed with a sense of adventure and taking full advantage of an open front door I was off, down the street half crawling and half staggering on my wee skinny legs, like a drunk man I headed for the Glasgow Road and freedom. The alarm was raised and a posse of frantic neighbours chased after me. I was finally captured by the search party only a few steps away from the busy main road and a close encounter with an SMT bus.

A wee gentle slap on the legs from my mum and a stiff warning about never doing that again and five minutes later I was out playing in the street again. The failed attempt only serving to encourage me to get it right next time.

All of us as children played happily together outside in the street, running around without fear of danger. These were the carefree days of traffic-free streets and close-knit communities. If my mum called us in for lunch and we were nowhere to be seen she knew that she would find us in a neighbour's house sitting at their table eating a jam sandwich with their family and on the other hand we often had a houseful of neighbours' children while their mums were out shopping or just to give them five minutes peace and quiet. Every neighbour was our family and every house was our home. Us kids didn't have much so anything we did have we shared between us.

If any child appeared in the street with a handful of biscuits we knew that soon they would be sharing them out among all the others. A bottle of tap water was passed around for everyone to have a mouthful, just a pity if you were last in the queue as the mouth of the bottle was covered with snot and all the crumbs and backwash from the others floated at the bottom of the bottle. We played games like kick the can, ring a roses, and of course us boys played football with an old can or any available round object whilst the girls played beds or skipping whilst chanting......

"Ring a ring of roses

A pocket full of posies

Atishooo...Atishooo

And all fall down."

We played outside from morning until the street lights came on. When it was raining we played in the closes or in the wash houses.

My personal favourite game, so I am told by my sister was a little more personal, peculiar and less sophisticated.

There were many dogs in our street, these were mainly strays, there was nobody who owned a pure-bred dog, which hung around scavenging for any morsel of food accidentally dropped by us children, often there was a scrabble and scuffles broke out between the odd mongrel dog and a hungry child over a dropped biscuit. Now naturally these dogs, not having the benefit of loving homes and proud owners had never been house trained and therefore answered the calls of nature whenever and wherever the notion took them. As a curious three year old I was magnetically drawn to these doggy defections and the urge to investigate them was far too strong for my tiny curious mind to resist. In the eyes of a scrawny wee three year old they had the uncanny resemblance to chocolate and as a makeshift toy gave me hours of innocent pleasure. I would sit on the ground fascinated by the squidgy substance and how I could squeeze it in my tiny hand and laughed hilariously as I closed my hand and watched it squidging through my wee stumpy fingers. Next I naturally had to give it the obligatory taste test. It definitely didn't taste like the chocolate that we used to find in our stockings at Christmas that's for sure, but as a substitute plaything it was brilliant I could rub it all over my face and clothes and have lots of fun making wee castles on the floor and spend time in innocent fascination by its consistency, until suddenly yanked up off the ground from behind by a screaming banshee of a mother who ,holding me at arm's length ran out to the back yard and into the wash-house where I was dumped unceremoniously into the big sink and held under the freezing cold tap while she scrubbed me clean with carbolic soap and the big, stiff, wooden scrubbing brush.

These houses were in poor repair, dank, cold and draughty, me and my sister continually suffered from colds, flu and chest infections.

The local council recognised the need to demolish them and to provide suitable modern alternative social housing for the tenants.

There were stories of a new council housing scheme at Castlehill and so my mum was off to the council offices on a mission to secure one of these luxury houses for us. My mum was an extremely strong, forceful woman who, when she decided on something nothing would stop her. So armed with the evidence of the poor, unlivable conditions, and her children suffering continual illness coupled with the story of my escape episode and first near death experience, she secured by charm, threats, or coercion the promise of a new house in Castlehill.

As the new houses were still under construction we had to stay a bit longer in Clyde Street. However, our Sunday treat was to get the bus to Castlehill and see how the new house building was progressing. We were awestruck with this fantastic, modern housing estate, with wide roads, we were pleasantly surprised to see that there were play areas specifically for children and that they were covered with grass, we were used to playing in the cobbled streets and concrete back yards of Clyde Street and had never seen grass play areas before.

There was even a parade of shops, with a newsagent, supermarket, and butchers.

These shops we would later discover were, Ian Cockburns, Jimmy Erskine Lusk's and Ian McGregor's these would be our local shops...all just for the families of Castlehill.

Finally after a few more months of waiting we moved to 6e, Carrick Terrace.

A top floor flat was our new home. The height of luxury, two bedrooms, a living room, kitchen and best of all our very own, private *INDOOR* toilet with a bath.

Castlehill was a result of the new prosperity coupled with the need to move families out of the dilapidated houses of Clyde Street and Denistoun and prepare the houses for long overdue demolition.

Castlehill, Brucehill and Westcliffe were the new social housing schemes on the west side of Dumbarton. The populations formed communities and there was an atmosphere of cheerful camaraderie. Adults gathered in the streets and communal gardens to pass the time talking and the children played happily in the play areas. You could leave your key dangling on a bit of string inside your letterbox and rely on neighbours to go in and check if you happened to be away for the day.

We quickly settled into this new life and forged friendships with the other kids on the estate.

Across the street was the Gren family with two sons and a daughter, my sister made friends with Ellen and Paul, Victor and I played happily together. Their father was Polish and had been a prisoner of war when he met their mother. He gave me the nickname Joe Pallooka. Just along the same street was the Junors two daughters Jessie and Fay were in my sisters group of friends. In Hawthornhill Road my group of friends was Mick Casey, Tom Robinson and Jim Reilly who were all my age and lived across the road.

Our quality of life had improved dramatically and all was going well until suddenly my dad became unemployed.

It was 1964 when Denny's shipyard closed and the whole workforce, including my dad, lost their jobs.

It was a bank holiday weekend and on Friday all the workers had their wages and looked forward to the long weekend, some would go to Glasgow to the Barras Sunday market, others to visit relatives, others just to stay at home and enjoy a couple of days to relax and spend with the family.

On Tuesday morning they all prepared to return to work, crowds gathered at the shipyard entrance. A closure notice was nailed to the main gates...they were closed never to re-open again.

Denny's were always innovators in fact the final project on the books was building a hovercraft, regarded by many as the sea transport of the future, so it was particularly sad that this once great, famous company was one of the first on Clydeside to go bankrupt.

The shock of this closure reverberated around Dumbarton and all the other shipyards on the Clyde held their breath. Many more firms would collapse over the next thirty years and I don't think that Dumbarton, ever fully recovered from the blow.

Of course all the connected industries, the steel forges and the iron foundries closed too.

Some men found jobs in other Clyde shipyards and others were too old to retrain and even if they could there were no jobs, so not able to travel to find work, they sank lower into despair and depression and either became alcoholics or simply gave up on life and died.

My father was one of the lucky ones and found a job as a delivery driver for Mason's furniture shop.

We lived happily in Carrick Terrace, my sister attended Notre Dame School and I had started school at West Bridgend Primary School.

My Grannie Gow lived in her, big, new house at 17, Caledonia Terrace,Brucehill and as both my sister's and my school were nearer to Brucehill,we always went to my grannies for lunch and after school ,only returning home to Castlehill at night.

Me and my sister were sprouting up and could no longer share a bedroom.

This two bedroom house in Carrick Terrace was just not big enough for our growing family.

This is what gave my mum the idea that we should move closer to my grannie and have a bigger house. So off she went to badger and bully the housing department of the local council for a move to Caledonia Terrace.

Our new home was 30, Caledonia Terrace, just across the road from my grannie, although it was almost next door we had all our meals and still spent all our time in my grannies house and again only went to our house to sleep.

But my mum was now happy and of course being next to my Grannie meant that she always had somewhere she could leave me and my sister while she went to the shops.

We practically lived in my Grannie Gow's house now that her family Frank, Danny, Tommy, Harry, Madge, and May had all married and only my Aunt Annie, Aunt Marie and my Uncle John were left at home.

Now that we were living in Brucehill I was allowed to walk to school without my mum with all my schoolmates from the estate.

New friendships were formed, and old friendships continued and I still played with my friends from Castlehill in school each day.

Family Matters.

We now lived in Caledonia Terrace at number 30, my grannie Gow across the road at number 17.

My Grannies house was an enormous, four bedroom house, due to the fact that when she moved there she had nine children, all still living at home. My grannie's husband, my granddad Francis Gow had died years before. He died at aged 51, which was about the normal male life expectancy in those days of poor healthcare, bad diet and dilapidated, damp social housing.

People died of tuberculosis, typhoid and smallpox diphtheria, and of course, lung disease. Most adults (and many children) smoked strong, unfiltered cigarettes, Capstan full strength or Woodbine were the most popular, They were referred to as "coffin nails", filter cigarettes had still not been invented, so consequently lung disease and cancer was common amongst adults and of course poverty was prevalent which resulted in high levels of infant mortality.

My grannie was born in Duke Street, Glasgow in the centre, next to Glasgow Cross next door to the prison. She used to tell us that when she was a child she could look out of her tenement 3rd floor window and watch the prisoners in the exercise yard and watched spellbound when the executioner arrived to carry out one of the frequent hangings.

The children used to play around the outside walls of the prison and sing……

There is a happy land

Doon Duke Street Jail

Where a' the prisoners stand

Tied tae a nail

Ham an' eggs they never see

Durty water fur their tea,

There they live in misery

God save the Queen

She left school at 13 and went straight to work in a clothes factory. This was quite normal in those days, as a wee Scottish girl it was a foregone conclusion that she would get married young and have children straight away. Young girls in those days didn't need much education, reading and writing were sufficient academic skills to prepare them for a life as a housewife. The families were poor and as soon as a child reached an age when they were fit and able to earn a wage to contribute to the family income, they were found menial jobs and left school. What my grannie lacked in academic education she made up for in worldly wisdom, and life experience, she had the ability to find a logical solution to any problem, and no matter how difficult or complicated it was. One of my grannies favourite sayings when I asked her how she knew the answers to my many questions about life was………..

"Acchh sure son, I never went to school….but I met a lot of scholars

So my grannie Mariah McConnell married Frances Gow, a shipyard worker from Dumbarton and they moved into their first house in The Vennel, a small, narrow street, just off the High Street in Dumbarton town centre, with already dilapidated houses, a room and kitchen with outside bathroom. The children arrived in quick succession, first came John, then Harry, Madge; Tommy, Mary, Frank, Danny, Marie and Annie. There was also another child James who died of Diphtheria when he was six years old.

In those days a vast amount of unfortunate children succumbed to terminal illnesses and never made it to their 10th birthday.

My granddad found work in Denny's shipyard and so they then moved to 13 Clyde Street. The street where all the houses were provided by Denny and Sons for their shipyard workforce who, for convenience, lived next to the gates of the shipyard.

So after my granddad died my grannie was left to bring up her large family alone. I often think about how difficult this must have been, living in those conditions through two world wars and struggling financially to feed and clothe nine children. My grannie was made of strong stuff, with a resolute character, and despite never having travelled, was worldly wise. She was the original "Iron Lady" and my hero.

She eventually moved to Brucehill and settled in her nice new modern house at 17 Caledonia Terrace. The house had four bedrooms, a new modern bathroom with a bath, and a living room with windows with spectacular, unobstructed views over the Clyde to Port Glasgow and Greenock. From the kitchen window, on a clear day you could see the Firth of Clyde. When it was my sister's turn to do the dishes, as the sink was next to the kitchen window and inspired by the stunning, breath-taking view she would belt out at the top of her voice and hopelessly out of tune...

Oh the River Clyde

The wonderful Clyde,

The name of it thrills me and fills me with pride.

And I'm satisfied that whate'er may betide

The sweetest of songs

Is the song of the Clyde.

The garden was enormous and all the sons spent their spare time digging and planting vegetables and potatoes. At the bottom of the garden was the obligatory Anderson Shelter. These were shelters which the council had built behind every house so that the families could protect themselves during the constant bombardment of Clydeside by the German Luftwaffe during the second world war .Clydeside was a strategic target not only because of the many shipyards turning out warships, aircraft carriers etc., but also for the aircraft factories where the engine and body parts for the war planes were built. When the sirens sounded that meant that a bombing raid was imminent so the families left the house as fast as possible, collecting only a few personal belongings and went to the shelter where they stayed, sometimes only a few hours, others a whole night, in this damp, cold hole in the ground, which was often filled with rain water and needed to be pumped out. They waited there in fear for their lives until the siren again sounded the all clear. If the house was hit by a bomb the theory was that the family would survive by sheltering in this inadequate, flimsy shelter.

The shelter was merely a tin shed with half of it submerged into a big hole in the ground and with a corrugated roof which was usually covered in dirt or grass.

I have serious doubts about the ability of a brick built shed with a tin roof to withstand the might of the German bombs, but I suppose the psychological advantage was that the family felt safe. My grannies house also had a Morrison Shelter under the house in the foundations. This shelter had an entrance from the rear of the house and the added advantage of an entrance from inside the house, which my uncles had constructed by removing some floorboards, and making a trap door in the hallway with a short staircase leading down into the cellar so it could be accessed easily during an air raid and someone could nip up to the kitchen and make a pot of tea between bombardments. When I was a child this cellar was a perfect adventure playground and as the old gas masks, oil lamps and other war paraphernalia were still there, me, my sister and our cousins and friends could play our imaginary war games. Later after the war the council came round and demolished all the Anderson shelters and boarded up the outside entrance to my grannies cellar, but as they didn't know about the secret indoor entrance we were able to continue with our games unhindered.

The house had a new modern kitchen, which my grannie called "*the scullery*", after years of cooking meals on the open fires in The Vennel and Clyde Street now the meals could be prepared on a new, fashionable gas cooker. In the kitchen there was a big pantry cupboard, which she called "*the scullery press*", and also in the kitchen was the coal cupboard, "*the coal press*". This is where the coalman Paddy Conroy would deliver sacks of coal every week to fuel the coal fire to heat the house and with a back boiler to heat the water. Paddy Conroy would walk in the front door, along the hall, through the living room and into the kitchen where he would offload his sack and empty it into the coal cupboard, leaving clouds of coal dust escaping and floating around the kitchen, whoever thought it was a good idea to locate a coal cupboard in a kitchen should have been forced to endure inhaling clouds of coal dust every time the sacks were emptied into the kitchen cellar. I remember watching this big strong man with a black face and hands and a leather apron walking through the house with a big, heavy sack of coal on his back, leaving black muddy footprints along the hall.

My grannie would always shout a warning to him........

"Noo don't you be giving me any of that dirty second grade coal...Paddy Conroy."

"If I'm paying good money for best quality I want best quality"

"No of course not Mrs Gow...I widnae dream of such a thing."

"And make sure you put in best grade I don't want to set ma hoose on fire with them sparks."

"Sure thing Mrs Gow you can trust me."

The coal fire was always lit in my grannies house and was the heart of the living room. I loved sitting in front of it feeling the heat on my face and watching how the flames danced and flickered with the light reflecting off the ceiling and walls. When the flames died, the luminescent, orange glow of the dying cinders transfixed me and I would stare at them until the black coal turned grey and my grannie would tell someone to throw some more lumps on the fire and the whole. Magical process would begin again. We all sat around it warming our feet and hands on cold winter days, just bad luck when Paddy Conroy had sneaked in some of his second grade coal and the gas pocket inside the coal ignited sending red hot coal shrapnel flying through the air in all directions. If one landed on someone's lap they leapt to their feet, spilling their cup of tea, dropping their cigarette and screaming and cursing about Paddy Conroy's cheap. Second grade coal. The roaring fire also doubled as a clothes dryer for my aunties' damp clothes and my uncles' socks were hung on the fireplace to dry when they came home from work on a rainy day.

My grannies house was always full, particularly on Sundays when all the family arrived for dinner. My Mum and Dad and me and Marie Therese, My Uncle Frank, his wife Ellen and my cousins Francis and Stephen lived in Dennistoun. My Uncle Tommy, Aunt Susan and Francis, Elizabeth and Susan, lived in Bellsmyre, My Uncle Danny Aunt Betty and Daniel, lived just round the corner in Kiel Crescent. My Uncle Harry, Aunt Agnes with my cousins Maureen, Harry and James all lived in Westcliff and sometimes my Aunt Madge who lived in Castlemilk in Glasgow and her daughters Marie, Marjory and Mary. My Aunt Marie later married a lovely we man from Govan called Tommy Bell, my Aunt Annie and Uncle John were still unmarried and living with my grannie, so there was always a full house, the kitchen was full of the women busily preparing the Sunday roast beef, roast potatoes and vegetables and the men sitting in the living room around the fire smoking their Capstan full strength cigarettes and talking about football and work while all of us cousins were sent outside to play "out of the way".

As no 17 Caledonia Terrace was in a crescent outside the front door was a grassy semi-circle where we played and which, for some unknown reason was called "The Triangle".

We were taught in geometry lessons in school about equilateral and isosceles triangles. Well this Mr Equilateral and Mr Isosceles obviously got their theories wrong and would have benefited greatly by visiting Caledonia Terrace and talking to us wee Brucehill children before embarrassing themselves with their stupid theories. It's no wonder I failed geometry in school. We were of course warned by our parents not to get dirty as we were all wearing our best Sunday clothes and to come straight in when we were called. With so many cousins we had to have two or three sittings for the dinner, arranged in chronological order oldest first youngest last. The big table in the living room even when fully extended could only seat 8 children or with a squeeze 10 or 12 We ate as fast as possible so we could get back out to continue our games of Kick the Can, Tag or Hide and Seek, while the adults ate their dinner in peace and quiet then spent hours talking and drinking copious amounts of tea from the big black teapot which was continually on the boil on the new gas stove in the kitchen and smoking their Woodbines leaving a dense cloud of cigarette smoke hanging in the air and coughing up their lungs. Later in the evening we all played cards or bingo and at 9 o clock ate the left over beef in sandwiches for supper. It was like the miracle of the loaves and fishes which we had read about in the bible. How we all managed to eat so much all day from so little still remains to this day a mystery to me.

The ritual changed when my grannie Gow got a television…..

It was Christmas 1959 and all the family had put some money together to buy my grannie a telly. In Brucehill we didn't know anyone who had a television. Televisions, like telephones and cars were only the privileges of the rich people who lived in the private houses in Oxhill or Cardross Road. So my grannie was one of the first to have this new invention in her house in Brucehill. It was a Pye and was a simple, square wooden box with a small screen. The controls were on the front, one knob to switch it on and another to change between the only two available channels BBC and ATV.

On the side it had three controls, horizontal hold, vertical hold, which were supposed to hold the picture steady and the fine tuning knob to locate the exact frequency of the signal, this last control was usually helped in its functionality by a good hard slap with the palm of a hand on the wooden side of the set, sending the wee ornaments my grannie had placed on top flying in the air. The small inside aerial had to be in exactly the correct position and would frequently need to be re-positioned during programmes resulting in a lot of cursing and swearing from all the family who were trying to watch a favourite programme. Later she ordered an outside aerial from her nephew Frankie Bell who climbed up on the roof and attached it to the chimney stack, then, with a chain of six people standing at strategic positions inside the house and one in the back garden, he manoeuvred the aerial into a position where the signal was strongest and the best quality picture was obtained. The person nearest the telly shouted stop when the picture was clear and the message was passed quickly along the chain to the one in the garden who then shouted up to Frankie Bell on the roof to secure the aerial in this optimum position. The process needed to be repeated often especially after a strong wind or storm dislodged the aerial and Frankie would be summoned urgently to reposition it again.

This T.V drew huge admiring, inquisitive crowds of neighbours to my grannies house.

In Brucehill at this time the front doors were only locked at night when you went to bed, all the neighbours were like family and in fact we called most of our neighbours aunties and uncles so any neighbour could simply walk in unannounced whenever they wanted for a wee visit and a cup of tea, They usually brought some snowballs, pancakes or cream cookies which they had just bought from Jimmy Gilies in the City Bakeries van in the street. So when the word went round that my grannie Gow had a telly everyone invited themselves in to have a cup of tea and marvel at this incredible new invention, coincidentally arriving just before the new series of Coronation Street or Emergency Ward 10 was about to start.

Of course there was absolutely no chance of all us cousins going to play outside now, when on a Sunday we could all crowd around the front of the T.V. pushing and jostling each other to win the best position in the front row to watch Champion the Wonder horse.

Our parents warned us that if we sat too close to the screen we would have square eyes but this warning fell on deaf ears as we were engrossed in the adventures of Champion or Lassie, The Lone Ranger, or Skippy the Bush Kangaroo. Later the adults shoved us out of the way so they could watch The News or Perry Mason, Private Investigator. The programmes all finished at ten o'clock with the national anthem then we would watch fascinated while the white dot in the middle of the screen finally disappeared a full five minutes after switching it off.

On normal week days I would run home from school to watch Jackanory or Thunderbirds, the Woodentops,Watch with Mother or, my personal favourite,

Bill and Ben the Flowerpot Men

*"Fluba duba dub. "*Said Bill

"Flubadub dubadub."...answered Ben

"Weeeeeeeeed"..... Said the weed

And spotty dog said ....*"woof woof."*

And they all ran back to the potting shed before Mr Green the gardener saw them.

This was educational, addictive, gripping stuff and I would run home from school as fast as my wee legs would carry me, jump the four front steps from the garden path to the front door in one mighty leap, swing the front door open.... clear the 5 yards from the front door to the living room door in 2 seconds.....throw my school bag on the floor and plant myself in front of the telly ......then listen as the front door finally swung closed.

I would sit on the floor in front of the roaring fire leaning back on my grannies chair with my grannie stroking my hair while she watched her favourite programmes. One of her favourites was The Black and White Minstrels, this was a group of singers and dancers who all blacked up their faces and disguised as black people sang all the old Al Jonson songs, very un P.C. in today's world and would be banned immediately. She would be out of her chair and standing in front of the telly with extended arms and singing along with the fake black singers......

"Mammyyyy....... Maaaaammyyy"...

"How I love you, how I love you, my dear ole Mammy"....

If it was the Andy Stewart or Jimmy Logan show she would be on her feet again dancing a wee Scottish jig around the living room in time to the bagpipe and accordion music. Her all-time favourite, however, and the highlight of her week was on a Saturday afternoon at 4 o'clock...The Wrestling.

She loved this sport and when it was Mick McManus or Jackie Pallo, her favourites, she would be out of her chair screaming and shouting and waving her walking stick at the T.V screen whilst threatening that if she ever got hold of that dirty wee bugger McManus she would kill him, while demonstrating the method of death by swinging her walking stick in the air in vicious sweeping motions. I made sure that I never sat next to her chair on a Saturday afternoon for fear of my life.

My mum would chastise her....

"Maw wid ye sit doon on yer bahookie ...you'll have a heart attack. Sure they're just acting."

"Whit d'ye mean acting? That durty wee bugger Mick McManus jumped on that poor wee man and was busy punching him in the face."

"No maw they only pretend to punch each other ….it's all fake."

"Acchh away and don't be so stupid May….and bring me a wee tot o' whisky to calm my nerves."

Sitting on the floor in front of my grannies fire watching my favourite programmes while she sat on her armchair stroking my hair is one of the happiest and most enduring magic moments of my childhood….with my grannie stroking my hair in front of the telly I didn't have a care in the world.

Another of my grannie's favourite pastimes was the horse racing. She just loved to bet on the horses. Every day she would study the racing pages of the Daily Record and choose a few horses to bet on. The form wasn't the most important aspect of a horse for her, her first priority in choosing the winner was the name of the horse, the second was the jockey. Her favourites being Lester Piggott and Willie Carson, if they rode her winner they were *"lovely wee men,"* but if her horse lost they were *"wee buggers from hell."* She would browse the racing pages and when she saw a name of a horse which corresponded with any remote connection to her enormous family, she would see that as a signal from god that she should put her two shillings and sixpence on its nose So, "Danny Boy", Tommy Boy, Frankie Boy, Mary's Dream, Lady Anne,…etc. were all worth a bet as she was sure they would win.

So she wrote out her betting slip and would send me or my sister down to Paddy Casey who was the bookies runner. He stood every day at the corner of Brucehill Road and Glencairn Road at lunch time and collected the bets of all the Brucehill residents. She would then position herself in front of the telly in the afternoon and avidly watch the racing from Goodwood, Aintree, Kempton or wherever that day's racing was being broadcast. On her feet with her walking stick in hand she would be screaming at the television, shouting the name of her chosen horse and cursing when it came in last.

I Made the mistake one time of jumping into my granny's chair when she was in her usual position, on her feet in front of the telly watching the day's racing and inadvertently put my hand down the cushion and leapt two feet in the air with shock .I had touched something cold, wet and horrible down the side of the cushion….

"AAaarrrrgggghhhh…whit's this in the chair?"…….. I screamed in terror

My mum came running into the living room to investigate the commotion…she looked down the cushion and laughed.

"Sure it's just yer grannies false teeth."

"Aaahhh." ….says my grannie *"I was wondering where they were and was just thinking about how I was going to eat my dinner with no teeth…..thanks for finding them son."*…..she said while inserting them straight back into her mouth.

Needless to say, after that shock I never sat in her seat again without first looking down the side of the cushion.

Most adults had false teeth. It was quite normal.

At around the age of 30 adults went to the dentists and had all their teeth removed, they then waited for a month or so until the new teeth had been made whilst enduring endless teasing and ridicule from friends and family who made them recite tongue twisters like "she sells seashells on the seashore" which, of course with no teeth was almost impossible.

Both my parents had false teeth and would leave them in a cup of water next to their bed or on the kitchen table when they went to sleep. I hated looking at these cups of teeth as there was always a crust of crumbs floating on the surface. The teeth never fitted correctly and would frequently rattle when their owners were talking or if in the middle of singing a song they simply fell out whilst their mouth was wide open and holding a note whilst vibrating their head. Most of this false teeth rattling took place at the many parties in my grannies house particularly at Christmas and New Year.

Christmas and New Year were the highlights of the year in my grannie's house.

My mum and aunties would spend days before Christmas and Hogmanay cleaning, shopping and preparing the house for all the many friends and family who would visit during the festive season. I never really enjoyed Christmas. My birthday is on 24th December and it was usually forgotten and lost in the turmoil in the hectic days of preparation, shopping, wrapping presents and cooking. I was always jealous of my sister because she had her birthday on 23rd May and so had the same amount of presents as me at Christmas and then again on her birthday, On her Christmas presents it said "Happy Christmas" whereas on mine was, "To Joseph, Happy Birthday and Happy Christmas"

New Year was my favourite. My grannies house was the venue where all the many family members gathered in the living room eating, drinking dancing and singing.

All my Aunts and Uncles and cousins would arrive during the day on Hogmanay laden with carrier bags full of bottles of beer and whisky for the men and Babycham or Advocat for the women, and enough food to feed an army.

The drinking and eating began early in the afternoon and by the time the evening came all the adults were all already in a very happy mood.

We children were sent out to play or told to run to Alec Robb's whilst the house was made ready to see in the New Year. This involved a lot of cleaning, borrowing extra chairs, cushions and tables from neighbours and sending us kids to Alec Robb's shop for any last minute shopping needed to ensure that the cupboards were stuffed full and overflowing. If the shop was closed we were ordered to knock on the side door, and keep knocking until Alec opened it and gave us everything which was on our list.

The kitchen was packed, my Uncle John was the chief cook. He had been a chef when he was a Franciscan monk in a monastery in Fort Augustus and wore his cooking apron all day whist baking fruit cakes with sixpenny bits hidden inside, and mountains of shortbread and with all my Aunties lending a hand to prepare the enormous amount of sandwiches required to feed the gathering army of relatives and friends.

As the party gathered momentum and with the noise level rising it was now time for the traditional "round the room" singing.

All the adults took turns at singing their favourite party piece songs.

My grannie would start off the singing with her particular speciality *"Wee Chookie Birdie."*

Wee Chookie Birdie to lo lo...

Laid a wee egg on the window sill...

The window sill began tae crack and wee Chookie Birdie went...quack, quack, quack.

Spurred on by the tumultuous applause and with shouts of "Gaun yersel Maw" she would then swallow another glass of whisky, get up from her chair and do a wee Scottish dance around the room while singing..."*Whistle, Whistle Auld Wife*" .....

Whistle, Whistle auld wife and I'll gie you a coo

Acchh....I couldnae whistle auld man although ye gied me two

Whistle, Whistle auld wife and I'll be your good man

Pheew, pheeew, pheeeeeewwww,

That's the best a can......

Next my Auntie Annie would slow the pace a little when she serenaded us with her current favourite....."*Sailor*"......

Sailor, stop your roaming

Sailor leave the sea

Sailor when the tide turns

Come home straight to me...

This always got the whole room waving their arms in the air and spilling their glasses of whisky all over each other while they joined in the chorus...

As you sail across the sea all my love is there to guide you,

In Capri or Amsterdam, Honolulu or Siam.

Then it was my Mum's turn.....

"C'mon May give us "Peerie Weerie, Winkle"...demanded the screaming audience.

My mum didn't need to be asked twice....she was on her feet........

She's my peerie, weerie winkle

My jeelie and my jam

My fairy, ma canary,

My bonnie wee bit lamb

She's ma bunch o sourocks

Ma laughin cockatoo

She's ma cockaleekie, ma cockaleekie loo.

In the gaps between singers even more sandwiches were passed round and there was a mad dash for the kitchen to refill the glasses…….

"Owen you're next but don't start yet my glass is empty"

My Dad always got everyone crying with his rendition of Danny Boy…..my grannie used to say that it would bring a tear to a glass eye………

Oh Danny boy

The pipes the pipes are calling

From glen to glen and down the mountainside

The summer's gone and all the flowers are dying

Tis you tis you must go and I must bide…

"C'mon everybody join in the chorus"…….

But come ye back when summer's in the meadows

Or when the valley's hushed and white with snow

Tis I'll be here in sunshine or in shadow

Oh Danny boy…Oh Danny boy…I love you soooooo.

This last elongated note was when all the loose sets of false teeth were catapulted across the room…then picked up from the carpet by their drunk owners who shoved them straight back into their mouths….then realized they didn't fit because they belonged to someone else.

My Uncle Harry's songs were my favourites and he had everyone in hysterics with his specialities……..

Three craws sat upon a wa

Sat upon a wa, sat upon a wa

On a cauld and frosty morning

The first craw was greetin for his maw

The second craw fell and broke his jaw

The third craw couldnae craw ata

On a cauld and frosty morning

Or.......

"The old barn door was the table we had and the table we had was the old barn door."

And.....

"Blue bells are blue bells...and blue bells are blue

These were the only lines in these songs and would be repeated for at least 50 times until everyone shouted for him to shut up and sing something different.

So he did....

OHHHHH a doo fell aff, a doo fell aff a doo fell aff a dyke

Oh a doo fell aff a doo fell aff a dyke... (Repeated 50 times)

"Oh for god's sake Harry shut up and gie somebody else a chance."

"Aye shut yer face an gie yer arse a chance."

The grand finale of the singing concert was my Uncle John who by now was drunk as a skunk and unable to get up off the floor he serenaded us with ...".My Grannies Heilan Hame,"

Whilst crying his eyes out then staggering off to bed......

Away in the highlands there stauns a wee hoose

And it stauns on the breast o a brae

Where we played as laddies a long time ago

Tho it seems it was just yesterday.

Oh the heather bells are blooming outside grannies door

Oh how I wish that I could see ...my grannies heilan hame.....

"Bbwwoooo hooooo hoooooo....I'm away tae ma bed."

After everyone had their turn singing it was now time for the Andy Stewart or Jimmy Shand records to go on and the settee pushed back against the wall to make space for everyone to get on the floor dancing, there would be more than 30 people in my grannies living room dancing highland flings and dashing white sergeants and then finally falling on the floor drunk.

All us cousins were sent upstairs to sleep sharing a big double bed, with all the boys top to tail in my grannie's bed and all the girls in my Auntie Annie's bed, of course nobody could sleep in my Uncle John's bed as he was already passed out drunk on top of it still wearing his apron. Naturally, it was impossible to sleep with all the noise from the party downstairs so we would lie awake telling ghost stories or sneak out and sit at the top of the stairs listening to our crazy, drunk parents singing and dancing in the living room bellow.

The adults wouldn't need the beds until the following morning when the party finished and we kids would then get thrown outside to play whilst they slept off the effects of the drink.

The following few nights were a repetition of the New Year party in all my uncles' and aunties' houses.

With the same ritual of singing, dancing and drinking continuing every night for up to a week later.

My Uncle John, my grannies eldest son lived with my grannie.

My uncle John was a very quiet intelligent man, although his chair was in front of the T.V. he hardly ever watched it except the news or the odd documentary. He spent all his time reading .He read The Scotsman newspaper every day. Now this paper was an enormous broadsheet and so when he was reading it nobody sitting on the sofa behind him could see the small T.V.screen. Nobody said a word, everyone simply all leaned to the side to get a better view around the sides of the paper. He was also an avid reader of books.

He had a cupboard in his bedroom which housed his enormous collection of books and in the cupboard on top of the stairs were even more. I was fascinated by these cupboards full of books, to me they were like Aladdin's caves and I would escape into them at every opportunity when my Uncle John was at work and hungrily devour information about every subject under the sun. He worked in Helensburgh as a telephone operator for the G.P.O. In those days with so few telephones if you wanted to speak to someone by phone you had to call the operator who then connected your line manually with the line of the person you wanted to talk to.

In his cupboards there were books on every subject arranged neatly on all the shelves,philosophy,psychology,science,biology,volumes of Encyclopaedia Brittanica,dictionaries,novels,poetry and of course, The Holy Bible all arranged neatly by subject.

I loved the musty smell of these cupboards and they attracted me like magnets, however, the one in his dark and dingy bedroom filled me with dread and fear. Going in there meant passing the scary painting hanging on his wall above his bed. It depicted Jesus Christ nailed to a cross suspended in space and looking down on the earth, his head bowed and blood flowing from his crown of thorns. This picture both intrigued and frightened me, I couldn't really understand the meaning of it, and it wasn't like the traditional paintings of Christ I had seen before in church or hanging on the walls of most Catholic's houses. I loved this painting but at the same time I also hated how it scared me. As a young, impressionable boy I was absolutely fascinated by this extraordinary painting and was uncontrollably drawn to it, sometimes going to the bathroom in my grannies house which was next to uncle John's bedroom I would open his door a little, stick my head round the door and just stare at the painting for a few minutes then run back downstairs as fast as I could to the safety of the living room.

When I was older, and studying art in secondary school I discovered this painting in an art book I was reading. It was called "Christ of St John of the Cross" and was by a Spanish painter called Salvador Dali who at that time I had never heard of but later grew to be my favourite surrealist artist. I loved my Uncle John's book cupboards, I would spend hours in them as often as I could devouring as many books as possible before my mum would shout up to me that it was almost time for Uncle John to come home from work and warning me that he better not catch me in his room, and to be sure to replace the books in their correct spaces or I would be in trouble. As I grew into a teenager and seeing me with my head constantly buried in books quenching my thirst for information about every subject, my Uncle John would often lend me books from his cupboards and answer my many questions patiently. Of course I couldn't tell him that I had already read most of them when he wasn't in.

My Uncle John was the first dead person I ever saw.....

He was only 51 when he died of cancer.

I was about 17 at the time he died. We used to have lunch every day in my grannies house. My uncle John was often ill and had recently had a serious operation where in an attempt to stop spreading stomach cancer he had half of his stomach removed, he never fully recovered and I am certain that he suffered a lot. One day while I was having lunch with my mum, dad and my grannie, my mum made a plate of soup and as my uncle John was confined to bed she went up to his room to see if he could manage to eat a little.

She came back down and opened the living room door slightly and not wanting to alarm my grannie she signalled to me and my dad to follow her. I was scared, I knew something serious was wrong and instinctively felt it was bad news, she whispered that she though he was dead and told my dad to bring up a mirror. In those days the test to discover if someone was dead was to put a mirror in front of their mouth and if there was no condensation they were definitely dead. We followed her upstairs to his bedroom, this bedroom which, for me had always been a source of fascination and fear. He was lying in bed on his back, I looked at his face, it was grey, his cheeks were sucked in and his lips were blue, his eyes were open wide and staring lifelessly at the ceiling his hands clasped over his stomach were also grey and the skin so thin that it appeared that at any moment his bones would burst through.

Although I had never seen anyone dead before ,to me it was obvious but my mum insisted on making sure with the mirror test ,what struck me most was that now he seemed so peaceful and calm. I was used to seeing my Uncle John doubled up and with pain etched on his face and now here he was lying peacefully on his back in his bed, his false teeth in a glass of water on the bedside table and with "Christ of St John of the Cross" looking down on him from space above his lifeless body.

Every time I see this painting I think of my dear Uncle John.

Although we only lived across the road from my grannie we spent more time in her house, not only because she had a telly but also my mum did most of the cooking and it made sense for us to have meals together in my grannies then watch some TV then go home, do our homework and go to bed. We had a radio in our house and we would sit at night before going to bed eating our supper of tea and toast and listening to radio plays or Scottish music by Jimmy Shand and his band on the light programme. Me and my sister always pestered my parents to let us listen to pop music but as the only music stations with pop music were Radio Luxembourg and Radio Scotland which were both pirate stations, meaning that they were broadcasting without a licence from boats at sea and were therefore illegal my mum was so scared that if we listened to them then we would be having a visit from the police or even worse, the S.A.S. would arrive and use battering rams to break down our front door and cart us all off to prison. She warned me and my sister about this major crime and so when we had our own transistor radios we would listen to them in our beds under our blankets, particularly on Sundays when radio Luxembourg broadcast the top 20.Later when we were older teenagers we had a "Dansette" record player. This was innovative, cutting edge technology as you could stack around 8 records on top and they would play automatically one after the other. This is where I listened to the first record I bought from Mullen's record shop in the Vennel...it was Ferry Across the Mersey by Jerry and the Pacemeakers.so we would spend hours just sitting listening to our own choice of music. Our parents gave me and my sister 5 shillings a week "pocket money" and we would spend 3/11 on a record each or put it together and spend 9/11 on the latest album.

My sister and I went to dancing classes when I was about 10 or 11 and she was 13 or 14

We went to The Agnes Stewart School of Dancing in Risk Street on a Saturday morning and learned the Waltz, Quickstep and Cha, Cha, Cha.

We became very good and entered many competitions and won our Bronze, Silver and Gold medals. Every time we had any visitors my mum would embarrass us by insisting that we show our guests what fantastic dancers we were.

So in the evenings and at weekends we would demonstrate our skills to all the family by pushing back the sofa to make space and putting on the Wheels Cha Cha on the dansette and dancing around the living room.

Later as teenagers this changed to the latest dance craze...*The Twist*.....

Ooohhh..... Let's twist again like we did last summer

Ooohhhh .....Let's twist again like we did last year

Do you remember when things were really humming?

Ooohhh ......let's twist again ...twisting time is here.

My dad was also an avid book reader, his preferred material was war stories.

My dad had been a soldier in the Cameron Highlanders.

At 19 years old he met my mum at a dance in the cooperative hall when they were both teenagers and their romance was just flourishing when my dad received his conscription papers.

On 6th June 1944 he, with his company, the 51st highland Division were captured by the Germans and taken prisoners of war. They were forced to march 60 miles to their first prisoner of war camp in Poland. He was kept prisoner for the duration of the war and made to work in the fields guarded by vicious German guards who would continually beat them with their rifle butts. My dad suffered permanent deafness in one ear after being victim to these continual blows. He never talked much about his experiences and after the war when he returned to Dumbarton he married my mum May Gow.Two years later 23 May 1947 their first child, my sister Marie Therese, arrived.

My dad's birth name was Own Mclean .He had no known family as he was adopted at the age of six months by an Irish couple, Joseph Mcloughlin and his wife Mary who, unable to have children they approached the convent where my father had been left by his mother when she emigrated to Canada, looking for a baby to adopt. My dad's birth mother gave the baby Owen to the nuns at the convent and asked them to find him a loving home. This was normal practice in those days. Teenage pregnancies were treated as scandalous, particularly in the catholic faith, and the resulting, unwanted babies left with nuns who would keep them and give them a good catholic upbringing until a new family could be found or simply sell them to rich couples with good homes in the U.S.A... So my dad was adopted by my granddad and grandmother Mcloughlin.I never got to know my paternal grandparents as my grandmother died before I was born and my granddad died when I was a small child. He was a strong man and although in his nineties was in good health, however, his liking for a wee drink was his downfall as after a night drinking in The Black Bull in West Bridgend he staggered out and crossing the road to go back to his house in George Street, Dennistoun he was knocked down by a bus and died from his injuries. He had a housekeeper and I remember visiting them on Sundays in their small dark house and sitting next to their coal fire eating ginger biscuits the housekeeper had made especially for our visit.

One of my enduring memories of my father is when, on a Saturday afternoon, he used to take me to football matches at Boghead to watch Dumbarton F.C getting beat again, or on other occasions to Parkhead to watch a Celtic match. I was never really interested in football but saw these occasions as the opportunity to spend time with my dad. Because I was so small he would lift me over the turnstile so I got in free and then send me down to the front next to all the other children to get a better view, and when a goal was scored he would grab me and hug me and throw me up in the air My father ,like most Scottish fathers in those days was not a tactile man, hugging and kissing was for sissies, so I treasured these precious moments and looked forward to half time when he would buy me a cup of hot Bovril and a meat pie. Even today when I smell or taste Bovril I am immediately transported back through time standing with my father, in the freezing cold on the terracing of Boghead or Parkhead.

My dad also loved walking, so on a Sunday morning when we returned from morning mass in St Michaels, and after we had eaten our big fried breakfast of square sausage, eggs, black pudding, beans and tattie scones, and we had finished reading the Sunday Post cartoons, Oor Wullie and The Broons, then he would take me and my sister on long walks while my mum crossed the road to my grannies house to prepare the dinner. These walks were often along the shore to Levengrove Park or in the other direction, The Scottish Rocks. This was an area of the Clyde shore between Brucehill and Cardross where along the shore were large rocks and stones. Me and my sister would run along the shoreline and discover interesting things which had been washed up by the tide, which we could then throw at each other. This filthy debris included, lumps of wood, seaweed, tin cans and any old rubbish discarded from the passing ships or deposited on the shore and collected by the tide on its route from Glasgow to Greenock, I was fascinated by the enormous cargo ships and oil tankers towed by tug boats which continually sailed up and down the river, and marvelled at the exotic names on the stern, .Cancun, .Aruba, Copenhagen, Hamburg, Ostend. Of course at this time, being only a wee Brucehill boy, I had no idea where these places were.

We would eventually reach the Scottish rocks and have a wee rest on the rocks before repeating the adventure by walking all the way back again. To us these Scottish rocks, which in reality were only a couple of miles from our home in Brucehill nevertheless seemed like the other side of the world. We would get home exhausted just in time for dinner.

Another of my dad's favourite Sunday walks was on the other side of Dumbarton.

The Long Crags is a range of hills which overlook our town and so we had to get the Silverton or Bellsmyre SMT bus from the bus terminus in Bontine Avenue in Brucehill. We always had to sit upstairs because my dad was a smoker, and I always pleaded to sit on the front seat so that I could pretend I was the driver turning my imaginary steering wheel when we rounded a corner and changing gears and braking to stop at the bus stops on our route. The bus took us to near the Dumbarton cemetery and then we would begin the long walk up past Overtoun House and through what we called The Witches Glen.......

"Do you see that big old house there son?"

"Aye daddy. Is it haunted...are there ghosts in it?"

"Aye son ...well that's the place where you were born".

"Why was I born there daddy? Did we live there daddy? Was it our house daddy? Were we rich daddy?"

"No son that was the nursing home where women went to have their babies."

"And yer mammy went there to have you."

I didn't understand all this baby being born stuff, and wasn't really interested, so carried on riding along the path on my imaginary horse.

This Witch's Glen scared the bejesus out of me and my sister. It was dark and dingy because of all the high trees blocking out the light and even on a sunny day had a creepy atmosphere. So we would walk along clinging on to each other for dear life with my sister telling me that she was sure she had seen a ghost floating above the ground just in front of us which would send me into hysterics. Then Marie Therese would run ahead and disappear into the woods and hide behind a tree then suddenly jump out in front of me with her arms in the air and her coat over her head and screaming wooohoooo, which had the desired effect of scaring me shitless and I would run screaming back to my dad, grabbing his hand and hiding behind his coat and pleading with him to tell my sister to stop doing that......

"Marie Therese you know he's a wee feartie so stop doing that."

"Ok daddy"....she shouted as she ran off to hide behind another tree.

There were rumours of a ghost called the Black Lady which haunted the woods, but we were with my dad and so we knew we were safe.

We would walk on up to the top of the hills through fields of cows which gave my sister another opportunity to tease me by telling me that they were bulls and that I should run as fast as I could as they only attacked and ate wee boys. Then she would watch as I ran as fast as my wee legs could carry me and falling over and landing with my face in one of the numerous cow pats whilst she doubled up with laughter and the docile cows continued munching the grass and ignoring the wee screaming eedjit in their midst.

At the top of the Long Crags there was an old concrete lookout post which was used during the second world war to keep a watch for any German planes or ships which might pose a threat to the town as the shipyards of the Clyde were a major target for the Luftwaffe and gunships and submarines often investigated there .This old brick built shed had amazing, panoramic views over all of Dumbarton and we could see the castle, the old disused Denny's shipyard, the River Clyde and the River Leven as it passed through the town centre, the prominent red brick building of Ballantine's Whisky distillery which was a distinguishing feature of our town. In the distance we could identify the nearby new housing estates of Bellsmyre, Silverton and in the distance, on a clear day our own estate of Brucehill and also Castlehill and Westcliff and across The Clyde to the towns of Port Glasgow, Gourock and Greenock. We spent hours up there with my dad who explained to us all the places of interest in Dumbarton while me and my sister climbed onto the flat roof of the shelter and stood leaning against the wind with our arms stretched out and seeing who could stay standing the longest before a strong gust of wind would send us flying off the edge straight into the waiting arms of my dad, then we would run around playing tag before finally sitting down on the grass and eating our spam sandwiches and cheese Smith's crisps with a wee blue bag of salt inside, and shared a can of Barr's Irn Bru which my mum had packed for us in a wee plastic bag, whilst my dad poured himself a cup of tea from the thermos flask he had carried in the deep pocket of his long gabardine overcoat.

Up the castle was another regular Sunday walk. We would walk through Levengrove Park, along the High Street and out the Glasgow road to the Newton or take a bus and get off at the Continental Cafe, cross the road and walk down past the ruins of now demolished Clyde Street where we used to live and past the gates of the derelict Denny's shipyard with my daddy telling us that is where he used to work as a hole borer. The castle had paths and stairs to reach the top but me and my sister preferred to climb up the rocks and run ahead and race to see who could reach the top first. At the top we would stand with my dad while he pointed out all the different parts of Dumbarton, and tell us stories of when we lived in the streets next to the shipyard. I was only 4 years old when we moved away from Clyde Street to Castlehill but could still remember the house and 13 Clyde Street where we lived.

The Brock Swimming baths at the common, was another favourite place of my dad's.

My dad was a good strong swimmer and so he decided when I was only about 5 years old that I needed to learn how to swim. The first time he took me was almost the last.

We changed in the cubicle and I was wearing my wee multi coloured swimming trunks that my grannie had knitted for me from leftover bits of wool and which when dry, itched my bum and my wee willy and when wet, usually dropped down to my knees.

My dad had the brilliant idea of tying them up with a bit of string which temporarily solved the problem until the string became loose and the trunks once again ended up around my ankles.

My dad told me to stand still at the side of the pool and wait while he jumped in and prepared to catch me.In my innocence and impatient excitement I only understood the "jump in" part of the instructions, so my dad dived in and while he was under water I quickly followed him, completely oblivious to the fact that I, of course, couldn't swim.

He surfaced, turned to the place where he had left me a few seconds before and was shocked to discover that I was nowhere to be seen. He looked around and could see my wee shape thrashing around under his feet, he reached down and grabbed my trunks and yanked me up. Well, these wee hand knitted, woollen trunks were not designed by my grannie to withstand such external forces and so as he raised his hand out of the water he was shocked to discover he was only holding a pair of wet woollen swimming trunks minus his son who, now naked, was still struggling for survival under the water and on the point of drowning. Diving under he managed to grab me and hoist me coughing and spluttering and gasping for air, out of the water.

After a stern warning about listening and doing as I am told the next time I was reunited with my multi coloured woollen trunks and continued with my swimming lesson.

The next time we went my dad had a brainwave. He had seen other children with these new inflatable plastic lifebelts. Being only made of thin plastic my dad decided that this was not good enough for his wee boy. His solution to keeping me afloat and therefore saving my life was to get hold of the inner tube of a car tyre, which he had discovered in the rubbish dump, and being made of strong, thick rubber was, in his opinion, an ideal lifesaving remedy.However,In his inventive excitement he had overlooked the fact that you can't blow the inside tube of a tyre up by mouth therefore we had to go to Buchanan's Garage in West Bridgend every time, before going to the baths, to inflate it with the compressed air machine. He also disregarded the fact that the nozzle for inflating it was made of brass and was on the inside rim where it could easily remove the skin and flesh from my ribcage. So now he was satisfied, and in his opinion, fully drown proofed and prepared for further swimming lessons with my woollen knitted trunks held up with string and my car tyre around my waist.........he was as proud as punch.... I was now ready to represent Scotland in the swimming events in the next Olympics.

Swearing by Almighty God

Religion, and in particular the catholic religion played a major part in my younger years. As catholic children we had religion continually drummed into our heads from parents, priests, nuns and teachers.

We were brainwashed and had to learn parrot fashion every prayer and repeat them from memory at school, at mass, at home. We were made to study the catechism and learn every question and answer. We could be stopped in the street by a priest at any time or he would arrive in our class unannounced and he would fire off a few random catechism questions at us and heaven help you if you didn't know the answers........

"Who made you?"

"God made me"

"Why did god make you?"

"God made me to know him, to love him and to serve him in this life so that I will be happy with him forever in the next."

"To whose image and likeness did god make you?"

"God made me to his own image and likeness"

"Very good Joseph ...you're a good wee catholic boy."

In school we had religious education morning, noon and night

We had to stand with our hands raised and joined together and eyes closed and face the cross above the blackboard before, during and after lessons.

We had religious education classes three or four times a day.

The priests could visit our schools and homes at any time unannounced, his collar was the key to every Catholic's front door, and give lectures about being good Catholics, going to mass, respecting our parents, teachers, adults and never ever under any circumstances must you touch your erect penis...this was sinful and a direct insult to god and you would burn in the fires of hell for all eternity

Whaaaat??....This was tragic news..... I loved touching my erect penis. This was very unfair, I loved how it grew and gave me a tickly feeling in my tummy. Why does god allow it to get hard, and why is it so much pleasure playing with it if we are not allowed to enjoy it?

We had to make our first confession and first communion when we were 7 years old. The girls dressed like mini brides and us boys in nice Sunday clothes and we paraded round the school playground hands joined and with a set of rosary beads entwined in our fingers, then into the church to go into a wee cubicle where the priest was sitting behind a screen and ready to listen to the heinous sins we children had committed for which he then forgave us. A couple of quick Hail Marys and Our fathers then into the mass to receive a wee round slice of bread which we were told was the body of Christ.

At 11 we had our confirmation, this is when we were officially accepted as Catholics and involved another dressing up day and another parade before entering into the mass and queuing up to be met in turn by the bishop who quickly slapped our face whilst saying prayers in Latin.

Of course at this early age we never questioned any of the rituals we were forced to perform, to us all this was completely natural.

These rituals, all the religious education, the strict rules and commandments which we had to follow set us apart from any other religion and surely proved to any Non-Catholic that ours was the true religion and that there was only one pope and one god...ours.

But of course this was far from the truth...there still existed people who didn't share our faith....they were called...Protestants.

I had very strict warnings from my parents not to play with, talk to or have anything to do with Protestants.

Protestants were the enemy. In fact anyone who wasn't a catholic was the enemy...but according to my parents,teachers,and the priests anyone who was of any other faith was at best misguided, deluded and destined to spend eternity burning in the fires of hell and needed spiritual guidance to help them to find the true religion which of course was Catholicism...and at worst the sons and daughters of Satan himself and were only on this earth because god had made a mistake and put them on earth to test the tolerance and virtues of us good Catholics.

Despite the stern warnings from all catholic adults and in particular my parents I made friends with a wee protestant boy called Robert Fincham who was about the same age as me.

My Grannie Gow lived at 17, Caledonia Terrace, and the Fincham family at 15 Caledonia Terrace and as far as I could make out apart from being Protestants seemed quite a normal family.

Robert and I made friends and played happily together most days after school and at the weekends. Funnily enough religion was never a topic of conversation for us and although he wore a different colour of school uniform to me, when we changed into our old playing clothes I couldn't see any difference. We played on our bikes, made gigs and kicked footballs around and we got on as children do, really well.

But my mum wasn't happy. Robert wasn't only a protestant but also a swearer, he swore a lot, maybe every second word. I loved this and of course copied him at every opportunity.

My mum threatened me with washing my mouth out with soap if she ever heard me swearing like that wee protestant and none of your mamby pamby jojoba and yucca perfumed variety, no, carbolic would be her preferred soap of choice for this torture. Carbolic soap smelled vile and could easily take the paint off doors. So with this threat hanging over my head I always made sure that all my swearing was done out of her earshot.

We planned our games of cowboys and Indians with the skills of a Hollywood director, all of us children knew how to direct as we spent every Saturday morning at the Rialto Cinema in Church Street at the minors watching the goodies John Wayne and the Lone Ranger riding through the wild west and killing the baddies.A goodie appearing on screen was met with screams of yeeeaaahhh...hoooooray...and the baddies with even louder boooooo s and whistles.

We even went dressed in our cowboy outfits we had got as Christmas presents complete with guns and cowboy hats. We knew every scene of every film including the dialogue by heart we even copied the American accents when we came outside

First we went to the Wrigley's chewing gum machine, put in our pennies, turned the big knob on the side and out came a wee packet of spearmint chewing gum....this was obligatory if we were going to be American cowboys..........

"Hey, +...let's saddle up and ride down to get some chow from Tony Biaggi's chip shop."

"Yeah Kimo Sabe...how far is it.?"

"Well I guess about a day's ride due east...we should be there by sun-up."

So off we went riding our imaginary horses down Church Street to Tony's chip shop,

tied up our horses to the wooden rail outside and swaggered in..........

"Whit's for you cowboys?"...said Tony

"Thrupence worth o chips and make it snappy pardner, we gotta get goin before the sheriff and his posse finds us."

"Yeah and put plenty of that salt n vinegar on there or I'll shoot ye between the eyes."

C'mon Kimo Sable let's get out of this town fast."

"Yeeeehaaaa...clickety clickety cluckety, cluck"

and we were off riding along the high street and up across the prairies kicking up clouds of dust to West Bridgend through Monument Valley to Dalreoch and up the Rocky Mountains to Brucehill.....arriving home just before sundown....

So Robert Fincham was a swearing machine.....

"Hey Joe....I'm the fuckin baddie and you be the fuckin goodie right and when I shoot ye ye fall aff your fuckin horse. Right?" ...said Robert
"Aye right and then I get up and run after ye and jump on yer fuckin back". ...I replied
"Naaa ya wee. Bastart ah ride ma horse away and you fuckin chase me"....answered Robert

I loved this swearing it made me feel really grown up. I was used to hearing swearing in school...everyone swore in school including the teachers.....

"Mcloughlin ya wee bugger...are you talking in my class.?"
"Nnnnoooo sir."
"You're a liar now get out here and put your hands out.".....slap, slap, slap, slap, slap, slap,
"Ahhh shit sir that hurt."

"What did ye say....did you just swear in my class.?"
"Nooooo sir."
"C'mon put them hands out again....I'll teach ye tae swear in my class ya wee shite."

I never heard my parents swear, they probably did just not in front of me or my sister. The strongest I ever heard my dad say was *"bloomin"* or *"blinking"* although my mum did use some stronger language from time to time like *"bugger"* although she always followed it with the sign of the cross and a *"may god forgive me"*

My sister had her swearing cupboard in my grannies house where she went when something earth shattering had upset her. Like being sent to Alec Robb's shop to buy 3 eggs and a tin of corned beef for tea whilst I was sitting undisturbed watching Champion the Wonderhorse. This injustice was just too much for her to take so she would go into the shoe cupboard in the living room and scream her obscenities at the Ewbank Queen carpet sweeper so nobody could hear her. Of course she would always get her own back later by giving me a sneaky slap when she thought my mums was turned

"Ouch. Mammy Marie Therese just slapped me". I'd scream

"No I never mammy he's telling lies again." She would say putting on her wee angelic, innocent face.

"I know hen he's been telling a lot of lies since he started playing with that wee Proddy bugger next door.".....*sign of the cross* *"may god forgive me"*

My sister was born with an incredible, natural talent......She could change her facial expression from devil to angel....in a nanosecond.

She would slap me while my mums back was turned and the second my mum turned round she was wearing the innocent face of an angel. She perfected this incredible trick and practiced it at every opportunity.

She would make faces at me and stick her tongue out whilst hiding behind my mum's back, which she knew would have the desired effect of annoying me and making me angry so I would try to get my revenge by kicking her, whereupon I would be on the receiving end again of a good hard slap for kicking my sister for no reason, and a lecture about not hitting girls, which pleased my sister no end with her covering her mouth and laughing or sticking her thumbs in her ears and wiggling her fingers whilst sticking out her tongue.......

"But mammy Marie Therese is still making faces at me behind your back."

"JOE!!!...Stop telling lies and making up stories to get your sister into trouble......and stop playing with that wee proddy next door."

The cliff was our playground, the Brucehill housing estate was built on top of a hill overlooking the River Clyde and the cliff was the part of the hill which was facing the river. It was red, sandstone rock about 50 feet high and was set at a 45 degree angle so us children could climb it, run around it and slide to the bottom ripping the backside out of our trousers. The cliff was our way of reaching the shores of The Clyde, there were stairs of course but we never used them, deciding that rolling forward or bum sliding down the sandstone surface was a much more exciting method, the stairs were only there for adults. It wasn't too dangerous because we were experts and knew every rock, bush and path on the surface, However being red sandstone it had the tendency to shed its surface and could be very unstable. Betwen the houses at Firth View terrace and the cliff edge was area of neglected, overgrown, waste scrubland. About 20 yards from the edge in the middle of this scrubland was a children's playground with swings, a slide, and a roundabout. Now I am not sure what genius town councillor had the brilliant, intuitive idea of planning a children's play area so close to a dangerous cliff edge………

"Well councillor McDougall, as head of planning and recreation department what plans do you have for creating leisure use for that unsightly piece of wasteland in Firth View Terrace in Brucehill?"

"Well Lord Provost, as we all know with the limited financial resources available to the council and with such a small budget for maintenance of this land I have decide to turn it to good use by building a children's play area."

"Excellent idea Councilor,this idea will save the council a lot of money in maintenance costs as the children of Brucehill, being juvenile delinquents, will play around that area flattening the bushes and keeping the grass low by setting fire to it."

"But does this not mean that we, the council will need to spend more money to install a safety fence, as the playground will be so close to the dangerous cliff edge?"

"No sir I have already thought of that, we only need to put up a couple of signs warning of the dangers of getting too close, and if any unfortunate child ignores the signs or simply cannot read and falls over then we are completely exonerated from blame."

"Absolute genius councillor. There will be a nice wee bonus for you at the end of the fiscal year."

The signs lasted two days, we soon discovered that if you swung on them from side to side they snapped at the base and then we could use them and as sledges to slide even faster down the face of the cliff.

One day me and Robert were playing one of our usual games of cowboys and Indians running around the bushes at the top of the cliff whooping, screaming and shooting at each other with our imaginary rifles and pretending to fall off our horses when suddenly wee Robert disappeared over the edge. I thought this was all part of the imaginary game and he was pretending he had been shot or he was hiding from me in the rocks, ready to jump out and kill me with his tomahawk….but when I went to look for him I discovered him lying at the bottom of the cliff spread-eagled and with blood pouring from his head. I slid down on my arse and helped him to his feet. He was ok and was acting brave until he realized that blood was pouring out of his head and starting to run down his face then he became hysterical.
"OOOhh Fuck….ohhhh shite…ohh ya bastard….ohhhh ya cunt…..ohhhh mammy daddy….oh mammy daddy. Oh fuck, oh shite, oh ya cunt."
This mantra he repeated continually between sobs all the way back up the hill towards his house.

"Don't worry it's only a wee scratch"…I told him as I replaced the flap of skin which was hanging down over his left ear.

"Ooo fuck…ahhhh mammy daddy, mammy daddy, oohhh Bugger…oohhh shite."

The Brucehill bush telegraph was working well and by the time we arrived at the top of the hill next to my grannies house, there was my mum, arms folded and with a face like thunder. The sight of her wee catholic son helping this swearing, blaspheming, protestant was just too much for her to take. Ignoring the bleeding, injured Robert, she grabbed me by the scruff of the neck and slapped me round the back of the head and legs whilst screaming that she knew something like this would happen and that she had repeatedly told me about playing with that wee proddy Fincham boy.

All this commotion had now alerted Robert's mum who had rushed outside to see what was happening at her front gate.

"*Arrrggghhh mammy mammy...arrggghh mammy*"... he had suddenly dropped the fucks, bastards, cunts from his vocabulary.

"*Whit's happening May?.....Whit has your son done to my wee Robert?*"

Sensing he could be in big trouble for playing on the cliff wee Robert immediately went into defence mode and told his mum that I had pushed him over the edge of the cliff and as a result now had a large chunk of flesh missing from his head.
Well this accusation, although false started the third world war between my mum and his mum, and soon my grannie and a few other neighbours came out to join in and take sides depending on their religion, in the biggest religious war since the crusades. With one side screaming abuse and the other responding likewise.......
"*You orange blooded protestants are the biggest liars on god's earth* "
"*Aye and you sanctimonious Catholics are all hypocrites going to your mass every Sunday then coming out and going in the pub tae get drunk*"
"*Aye but at least my wee Joseph disnea swear like a trooper like your Robert.*"
"*Aye but your holy wee catholic son pushed my wee Robert over the cliff*"
"*Well I don't believe he did cos your wee Robert is as big a liar as you and if he did he should have pushed the wee bugger harder and if he didn't then he damn well should have.*"*sign of the cross* "*may god forgive me*".

Meantime poor wee Robert was being ignored and still with blood continuing to pour out of his open cut and running down his face we sneaked around the back and sat on the stairs to wait for the hostilities to end and for someone to clean him up and put some kind of bandage round his head. I couldn't help noticing with surprise that the blood seeping out of his head was of course not orange as my mum had claimed and was actually red and pretty much the same as mine.

Soon after this incident the Fincham family moved away and were replaced by a good catholic family the Dobbins. A big family with Mr and Mrs Dobbins, Grannie Boyle, an Aunt Nanny and four children, three boys, Andy the oldest, Pat, the same age as me and George, who was the youngest. The only daughter Mary Cyra was born there with the help of my Grannie Gow, who doubled as the local midwife and "layer out". The layer out was the person who visited the house when someone died and washed and dressed the bodies in preparation for the visitors who came to pay their respects...

The Dobbins boys were my new friends and playmates and swore like troopers, even more than Robert Fincham.My mum was now happy that I had good wee catholic playmates who wouldn't be a bad influence her wee innocent son.

For me swearing was a sign of my maturity, when I swore I was a "big " boy and although I had been told it was a sin it never really bothered me too much because I also knew that I could go to confessions on Saturday and come out with my soul clean again. Confessions for us Catholics, was like going into a washing machine, you went in with stains on your soul and came out nice and shiny, fresh and clean again....ready to start the sinning all over again.

"*Bless me father but I have sinned it has been one week since my last confession.*"

"*I was cheeky to my parents.... three times*"

"*I fought with my big sister... five times*"

"*I swore.... three times* "

"*And I told lies*"

"Very good my son...but how many times did you tell lies?"

"Well father including the one I just told you about swearing......seven times."

"Now my son now say an act of contrition and for your penance say three Our Fathers and seven Hail Marys."

Lucky for me I missed out the bit about touching my wee erect penis or I would have been wearing sack cloth for a month.

As we grew into teenagers my sister and I were warned continuously under threats of death, about making sure we never had any romantic inclinations towards any protestant boys or girls and under no circumstances should we ever consider bringing any non-Catholic home to meet our parents.

To be fair I am certain that the same warnings were delivered to the teenagers of protestant families too.

It was obligatory for Catholics to marry Catholics and mixed religion marriages in my town were very, very rare. If a catholic boy or girl married outside of the catholic faith then they were immediately excommunicated from the Catholic Church and of course also excommunicated from their family. The family was ashamed and turned their back on them.

Of course these enlightened days this seems barbaric I am happy to say that mixed faith, mixed race, same sex marriages are normal. I am of the opinion that love has no faith, religion, colour or gender.

Me and my sister were lucky to be teenagers during the 60's...the sexual revolution was underway and I being a typical teenager personally took full advantage of the free sex, peace and love generation. I couldn't have cared less if a girl was catholic ,protestant, atheist, black, yellow, green or had two heads...if she was up for a shag ...I was in.

If Protestants were enemy number one, then a close second was the English...so an English protestant for example was a double whammy.

Curious then that both me and my sister ended up married to English Protestants.

My sister suffered more than me, as three years older and very attractive, blonde and trendy my sister had lots of boyfriends. Like me she was more interested in the person rather than their religion and on occasion she would be seen by some nosey neighbour with a protestant boy, through misplaced loyalty the neighbour would tell my parents and she would be warned, under threat of death by stoning, never to see that boy again.

We were encouraged to go to the dances and discos in St Michael's church hall where we would mix exclusively with Catholics, However we preferred the burgh hall dances where all the town teenagers went.

The burgh hall was in the centre of the town and on Saturday night in our small town was the only place to go meet the opposite sex. Us boys would first go to the Elephant and Castle pub, which was the only pub where no questions were ever asked about your age, if you could reach the bar you could buy a drink. So after a few pints of heavy in there we would buy a couple of bottles of cheap wine called Eldorado and share them down the quay before entering the burgh hall. There we could dance with Protestants, Catholics or whoever we fancied and if lucky have a snog...or a lumber.

Any non-Catholic girl you walked back to her house of course had to stop a long distance from her gate as her parents or neighbours would be watching to see who walked her home.

The next day my dad, looking at me over the pages of his News of the World would interrogate me about the night before......

"Aye son how was the dance in the burgh hall last night?"

"Aye fine daddy it was great."

"And did ye get a lumber?"

"Aye daddy...I lumbered a wee lassie from Castlehill."

"I took her doon the quay and shagged her then I shared her with all my mates and we drank Eldorado and injected heroin and sniffed cocaine …. I think one of us made her pregnant."

"Ach aye but is she a good catholic?"

"Of course daddy."

"Aye that's fine son...ye can bring her home anytime."

Discipline

We were children we needed discipline. This was an undisputed fact of life .This discipline came in many forms but usually consisted of some form of physical punishment which we were told we needed to make men of us and was character building. Of course girls were also the victims of discipline but normally at home it was more verbal than physical. However, in school it was a different story.

My sister went to Notre Dame School and was taught by nuns. Now you would imagine that being nuns their gentle character, righteous virtues and belief in god would prevent them from dishing out corporal punishment to small children, but no. These "Sisters of Notre Dame" nuns were vicious psychopaths and thought nothing of using the strap on some poor wee innocent girl who happened to be late for school. I think they misinterpreted the passage in the bible which says suffer little children to come unto me.

This was a time when respect for adults and in fact anyone in any position of authority was paramount.

Any breach of the many complicated rules was met with physical violence.

In my secondary school it was a weapon of mass destruction called the strap, a big, heavy lump of leather about 2 feet long with two tails. Our teachers wore this instrument of torture like a badge of honour and were happy to use it on the extended palms, knuckles or heads of any child who, in their opinion, deserved it. The offences punishable by this barbaric method were endless and the ratio of punishment to crime was only determined by the mood and character of the teacher.

We expected it for offences like speaking in class, not doing homework on time, eating, drinking or breathing without permission........

"Mcloughlin!!!"

"Yes sir?"

"Are you listening to me?"

"Yes sir"

"What did I just say?"

"Errrmmm.....are you listening, sir!!"

"Get out here now boy"

"Put out your hands"

"Slap, slap, slap, slap, slap. Slap"

"Now get back to your seat and don't be so cheeky in future"

Now these slapping really hurt and often my hands and wrists would swell up and turn red raw. If the teacher was a bit short sighted he often missed the target area and only caught the edge of your hand so in the interest of balance you got an extra slap. Of course this rule also applied if you pulled your hands back or moved them to the side. The important thing was not to cry or show any sign of weakness in front of your classmates. Also very important was to pray that the swelling disappeared before I went home, because if my mum saw it and knew I had the strap I would get another good slap on the legs for getting the strap. These slaps from my mum would be accompanied by endless questions. Each question was allocated a slap for every word or sometimes every syllable if it was a long word. There was never a fair trial on these occasions and any attempt at an explanation was futile. The best idea was for me to accept this punishment without arguing as any form of reply was considered cheeky and insolent and would result in extra slaps........

"What's that mark on your wrist? Did ye get the strap at school?"

"Aye mammy"

"C'mere ya wee tinker."

"Whit"- slap "did"- slap "ye"- slap "get"- slap "the" – slap "strap"- slap-"for"- slap.

"Mr Quigley said I wasn't listening in class mammy."

"How"- slap "many"- slap "times"- slap "have"- slap "I" slap "told"- slap "you"- slap "about"- slap-"list"-slap "en"-slap-"ing"-slap "in" slap-"class"-slap.

"Now let that be a lesson for ye."

"Aye mammy."

"Noo away ye go and do your homework and listen when the teacher is talking in future."

"Aye mammy."

My mum was the punisher in the family. My father was a very quiet peaceful man and when I needed (or not needed) any discipline it was always my mum who ladled it out.

"Owen, for god's sake talk to that boy."

"Aye right May"…."hello son, how's it going"?

"Aye fine dad...and you?"

"OWWWEEENNN!!!!"

My mum was also blessed with an amazing memory, so if I had committed some punishable offence and she was too busy, cleaning or making the tea to administer the prescribed slaps she would remember later and give retrospective punishment.

I remember when I was at primary school and my teacher Mrs Connolly gave us homework to write an essay about the Loch Ness Monster. I loved writing essays and with my wee active mind buzzing with ideas I would let my imagination run free. When Mrs Connolly read my essay she made me stand out in front of the class and read it out loud to the rest of the class. She told me it was brilliant and gave me an "A" star and stuck it on the wall of the classroom. I was so proud of myself and ran home to tell my mum….

"Mammy, mammy...Mrs Connolly said my essay was fantastic and I got a gold star."

"Ohhh that's smashing son."

"What did ye write about?"

"Oh it was about the Loch Ness monster."

"Ahh sure that's great son ...I'm very proud of you...now sit at the table for your tea".

One day about three weeks later I came home from school as usual, sat down on the chair and started to do my homework, when my mum appeared with a face like thunder and slapped me hard across the legs....

"Do you know what that's for?"

"No mammy"...

There was no point in trying to think about what breach of the rules I had made recently...I knew from experience that the reason for the slap was coming soon.

Well she continued..."*I met Mrs Connolly, your teacher, today in the street and she told me about that essay you wrote about the Loch Ness monster."*

"Aye the one she gave me the gold star for."

"Well ya wee tinker ye never told me that ye wrote that the monster wriggles its bum in the water like Jane Mansfield the film star"...slap, slap, slap.

"But mammy...Mrs Connolly told us to use our imagination...so I did....and Mrs Connolly said it was fantastic."

"Aye well ye gave me a right showing up in front of yer teacher ya wee tinker...I was mortified"......slap,slap,slap.

Of course your immediate family weren't the only adults with punishment privileges.

There was an enormous list of authorised slappers. Almost any adult, relative, distant relative, friend of the family, neighbour...etc., etc. was empowered with the right to dole out any slap or other punishment they saw fit for the crime.....

"Mrs Mcloughlin yer wee boy kicked his ball into my garden today...I had to give him a good, hard slap to teach him a lesson."

"Oh that's very nice of ye mister. He must have deserved it."

"What's yer name?"...."*I'll put you on the list."*

My mum had her favourite threats which ranged from ......*"I'll break yer jaw* "to *"I'll rattle yer teeth* "to *"I'll draw my hand across yer face"*

But my favourite was *"I'll cut yer legs aff "*

This last threat was reserved for serious breakage of the rules and major crimes like not coming in for dinner when she called me.

"JOE!!!"

"Yer dinners ready come in"

"Aye in a wee minute mammy, were finishing our game o fitba."

"Come in now or I'll cut the legs aff ye.....ye'll never play fitba again."

I often wondered how she would carry out this procedure.

Would she wait until I was asleep the creep in and cut through the flesh and bone with my dad's saw or simply use the big axe my dad used for cutting firewood?

This threat always scared the life out of me, even more when one day I saw Wee Mr McClure.

Wee Mr McClure lived in our street and he had no legs, just two stumps where they used to be.

There were many cruel jokes told about the legendary wee Mr McClure.....

"I saw wee McClure coming out of the Burgh Bar last night."

"Aye did ye?"

"Aye ....he was legless."

"See that wee McClure....well he's nothing but a low down bum"

"Wee McClure is in the Olympic Games next year"

"Eh...how come?"

"He's entered the LOW jump....he's sure tae win the gold medal"

The first time I saw this living Brucehill legend I was frozen to the spot.

I was coming home from school one day kicking an empty Tennants Lager can along the pavement in Caledonia Terrace when the can landed at wee Mr McClure's gate. As I crossed the road to collect it there he was, the man himself. He was coming down his front path using his hands as crutches and swinging himself forward to get to his front gate. I stood there with my mouth open.

"Hello son"

"Could ye open the door of my car please?"

"Err...Err...Err sure mister."

MY car. He said **MY** car how he could have a car when he hasn't even got any legs.

He swung himself with ease into the driving seat of his Morris 1000, closed the door, started the engine and drove away along the street.

What I had just witnessed was nothing short of a miracle. So many questions went through my young inquisitive mind.

How could he possibly drive a car with no legs?

At eight years old and even with a limited knowledge of the mechanics of cars I knew that the minimum requirement was at the least two legs preferably with feet attached and two arms, and here was wee Mr McClure driving a car with no legs and moreover no feet..

The answer came from my grannie Gow when I ran into her house and breathlessly explained the miracle I had just witnessed.......

"Grannie...grannie....I just saw that wee Mr McClure driving a car...and grannie he hasn't got any legs...How grannie?... How can he do that?"...

"Ach away aff ya silly wee boy."

"Sure he's got wan o them specially adapted cars he can drive with his hands."

"Aye Granny but how can he make it start and stop and turn the wheel at the same time?"

"Ach away an ask yer dad and stop bothering me with yer silly questions."

Every day I passed his gate hoping to witness his incredible car driving exhibition again.

Poor wee Mr McClure was the victim of many cruel pranks.

One of our favourite street games was K.D.R.F.....Kick Door Run Fast.

The object of this amusing pastime was to knock on someone's front door and then run away as fast as possible so that when they opened the door nobody was there, then five minutes later return and do it again.

Well of course being heartless, twisted minded, little buggers we played this sadistic, annoying prank on wee McClure.There would be a queue of children outside his gate waiting to knock his door and instead of running away just waiting around for 10 minutes, casually chatting until he eventually opened the door. Then calmly walking away, safe in the knowledge that he couldn't chase after us.

"Ya wee Bastards", he would shout.

"When I catch ye I'll kick yer fucking arses".

Obviously it slipped his mind for a second that he lacked the two essential requirements to carry out this threat.

There were many questions I needed answered not least how did he lose his legs in the first place.

Various reasons were put forward, one that he was a war hero and had stood on a landmine and got his legs blown off.

Another was that he had frostbite and had to have them amputated.

Yet another was that he was born without legs.

This last reason baffled me most because surely if he had been born without legs someone would have noticed and they would have kept him in the hospital until they grew on.

My own personal theory was that his mother had called him in for his dinner when he was a wee boy while he was playing football........and he came in late.

Crime and Punishment

As young children growing up in Dumbarton we didn't know much about crime. Dumbarton, at this time, was a very safe, low crime area .Of course we lived in different times when there were sufficient deterrents in place to prevent crime, such as, long prison sentences in tough prisons, or just a hard slap round the head by the local bobby who warned that he would be telling your parents if you so much as breathed in the wrong direction. He was a figure of fear and walked around the streets as if he owned them. He knew every family on his beat and could be your friend or foe, depending on your behaviour. There were no brain dead judges or hand-wringing lawyers crying about human rights, your human rights in those days ended when you committed a crime.

Of course we were just normal, mischievous youngsters, not exactly angels but our petty crimes extended to stealing apples from the orchard in the Kiel school, an activity we thoroughly enjoyed and approached with the tactics of an SAS raid.

The Kiel school. Or "The Keely" as we knew it was a large private boarding school for intelligent, posh kids from rich families. I'm sure that they must have been very happy to discover that their equally posh school was next door to one of the toughest council estates in Dumbarton, namely Brucehill. This school and its extensive grounds complete with orchards and rugby fields was just too much of a temptation for us mischievous kids. It was surrounded by a six foot fence and in some places a six foot wall with broken glass cemented on top, however, this never really proved to be any sort of deterrent to us. We would climb the wall using any old bit of carpet or cardboard to cover the glass or remove some of the uprights of the fence, squeeze through and post a sentry whose job was to watch for the caretaker or any other adult approaching. The signal was a whistle or a copy of a bird call to alert us up the tree that it was time to jump down and run for the wall with our jumpers full of apples. These we would then devour until we had stomach-ache or we would throw them at each other or anyone who happened to pass our hideout. We obviously couldn't take them home because our parents would know that we hadn't bought them, because us kids never had any money, so by the process of elimination the conclusion would be that we had stolen them and the punishment for stealing was of course a severe beating with any heavy object which came to hand.

In my teenage years during the 60s the crime level increased with the introduction of gangs. These gangs were the normal culture in most cities in Scotland and particularly in Glasgow's tough housing estates such as Drumchapel, Maryhill, Castlemilk and Easterhouse. In these parts of Glasgow the gang violence was extreme, with regular gang fights and stabbings, shootings and murders with gangs from each area or even from opposite ends of the same estates fighting battles to the death. They would use any weapons they could get their hands on, knives, hatchets, chains, wooden or metal poles, or even the odd meat cleaver stolen from the local butcher shop. They would fight these wars in the local streets and put the fear of death into all the local residents.

Dumbarton had its own watered down version of this in the council estates like Castlehill, Bellsmyre and of course my estate Brucehill.The main rivals were the gangs from outside Dumbarton like Helensburgh, Balloch, Renton and Clydebank.

If the gangs couldn't find a fight with gangs from outside the town then they would simply fight amongst themselves.

The big danger here was that as Dumbarton is a small town and our school catchment area included the surrounding towns in Dunbartonshire, many of these gang clashes happened in or outside our school, and later when we left school in the regular dances on Saturday nights in the Burgh Hall. The Burgh hall was our centre of entertainment and every Saturday night we had dances with live music from Glasgow bands like The Beatstalkers, The Poets, Dean Ford and the Gaylords or The Pathfinders. These bands were the most famous bands in Scotland in the sixties and in fact Dean Ford later changed their name to Marmalade and found national success. They always had hordes of adoring, teenage fans who followed them around and which gave us boys a fresh selection of female talent to ogle. The music would be loud, just as we liked it and the songs of the time would have us all up dancing……

Na Na Na Na Na

Na na na na na na na na

na na na na

Know how to pony...wooooyeahhh

Bony maroneyyy ohhh yeahhh

Do the mashed potatooooooo...ohhh yeahhh

Groovy alligator....ohhh yeahhh

na na na na na

na na na na

na na na na na na

These dances would start off very peacefully with everyone having a good time, dancing and chatting up the girls when suddenly an outside gang would arrive from maybe Clydebank, Helensburg or Balloch then all hell would break loose when they were challenged by the local Dumbarton gang called "The Dinky "

There was also"..."The Young Dinky"….and "The Young, Young Dinky"….I think there might have been a "Foetus Dinky" too …but I'm not sure.

These gang fights, similar to bar brawls in the films of the Wild West, would continue without interruption until the police eventually arrived, when those who were still alive and breathing running off and being chased by the police and the survivors being carted off to hospital to be stitched up. The scars of these gang battles were worn by the victims like war medals and a lot of boasting was done about the fights, always exaggerated beyond the realms of fantasy…….

"Whit's that bandage on yer heid son?"

"Oh that's nothing….jist a wee scratch, 50 stitches, I got in a fight in the Burgh Hall last Saturday."

"Oh aye whit happened."

"Well I was just dancing and mindin my own business when a gang of about 20 boys from Helensburgh attacked me"

"Oh my god, a gang of twenty thugs from "The Beach Boys" attacked ye???

"Aye but I jist picked up a chair and got stuck intae them all"

"All the 20 are in hospital. Two are critical. And four are in comas."

The big problem for us young Dumbarton teenagers was that all the best nightlife was in Glasgow, The Maryland, in Scott street and The Electric Gardens in Sauchiehall Street were just two of our favourite clubs and of course travelling to the city on a Saturday night was fraught with danger, as teenage boys from Dumbarton we had to run the risk of being attacked in the street or even inside the clubs for nothing more than looking at someone or god forbid, dancing with a girlfriend, ex-girlfriend, sister or neighbour of a Glasgow gang member.

This ever present danger never really bothered me, I was never a fighter but I was a good runner, my dad always told me......

"Son with that skinny body and them long, skinny legs you will never be a fighter, so if I were you son, I would practice running,"

Also I was never a member of any Dumbarton gangs so I could more or less move pretty freely in most parts of the town only being chased on a few occasions when for example, after the dances in the Burgh Hall I took home a girl from Bellsmyre then when I kissed her goodnight and left her at her door I would run as fast as I could to get off the estate before being spotted by any of the local gang members.

The most frightening incident I can recall was when I was about 16, I was a mod and of course I had the obligatory mod scooter, a red Vespa 160 GS the ex-army parka with fur collar, Fred Perry shirts, hush puppy shoes etc.I kept well out of trouble, my scooter was my love and my life and I had scooter friends Puggy Peters Peter Deeny, Bobby Murphy and Tom Robinson and also in Helensburgh and Balloch and we were happy riding our scooters and not getting involved in any gang wars. This friendship with other mods is what I´m convinced saved my life.

We used to go on Saturday nights to the Maryland nightclub in Scott Street in Glasgow, it was a soul and RnB club and not only attracted mods but a mixture of the type of teenagers who liked the current vogue for soul and blues music. Of course all of us boys had to be searched by the doormen before being allowed in, to make sure that we weren't carrying any weapons. The gang's members were always one step ahead and as the girls were never searched they simply gave a girl a weapon to put inside their handbag, later once inside to be passed back to the gang member. I was wearing the obligatory new double breasted suit jacket, my checked, hipsters, hush puppy boots and my Ben Sherman shirt I really did look the dog´s bollocks. I was happily dancing with a very pretty girl and impressing her by doing all the best dance moves when suddenly I felt a heavy hand on my shoulder and I was spun around to come face to face with a very big, tough looking angry gorilla who, without any form of exchange of pleasantries or introduction stuck a knife at my throat and told me in no uncertain terms that he had already warned me on several occasions that dancing with this girl was a big mistake and that, as all his previous warnings had obviously been ignored, he was now going to stab me in the neck. I was completely frozen to the spot and trembling with fear.

Now, I had seen people stabbed in the neck before, there was always a fountain of spurting blood and accompanied by screams of pain not to mention the slow agonising death from excessive blood loss which followed this violent non-surgical procedure.

My pretty dancing partner was trying to explain to this Neanderthal ape-man that he had made a terrible mistake and that as all these" fucking mods" look the same that I was indeed not the same "fucking mod" to whom he had issued his death threats on several previous occasions.

Now this overly aggressive thug was having none of these explanations or excuses and his knife was still only a centimetre from my carotid artery and with all the pushing and shoving going on around us in this crowded club coupled with the crazed look on his face I was saying my last prayers and silently bidding a last goodbye to my family, my scooter and all my friends and my short life was about to come to a sudden and excruciatingly painful end. He was hell bent on murder, in particular, my murder and I was surely going to be his next victim, the next notch on his knife. I had a fleeting vision of my imminent demise, me laying on the floor in a pool of blood, my body still twitching in its death throes, while he stood above me, knife dripping with blood,…my blood,… head held high and laughing like the madman he surely was, proud that he had put an end to this insignificant little skinny mod who had the audacity to disobey his orders and disrespect his authority by dancing with his girl, and all while Johnny Johnston and the Bandwagon were singing Blame it on the Pony Express in the background. I closed my eyes for what I was sure would be the final time and waited for the onslaught of pain and the following oblivion of certain death.

After a few seconds of nothing happening, curiosity got the better of me and I slowly open my eyes .His ugly, twisted face had disappeared from my view and without warning he was suddenly on the floor having being punched square on the head from behind by one of my mod scootering friends from Helensburgh, who then picked him up and holding him by the throat told him he had made a mistake and that I indeed was a small fry, timid cowardly skinny, insignificant little shit and that he should save his energy and knife for later when he surely could find a more deserving mod victim to put to death.

Needless to say I grasped this opportunity, and with a nod of gracious thanks to my saviour, I was out of that club faster than you could say "Quadrophenia".

It was on the last train home from Glasgow when retelling this terrifying, near death experience to other friends that I discovered that my attacker truly was a knife wielding maniac from Helensburgh who was well known amongst the gangs in the town as a murdering psychopath who in no circumstances should be messed with. I was informed that I had indeed escaped an excruciatingly painful certain death by seconds.

 It was a couple of weeks later on another Saturday night en route to Glasgow for the usual night out and having recovered from my death defying experience that me and a couple of my mod friends were waiting at Dumbarton Central station for the train to Glasgow. The train arrived and as we happily got on and in our usual high spirits sat down and relaxed for the half hour journey to Glasgow. I looked across the carriage and froze with fear, the blood drained from my face, my heart was pounding as if it was about to jump out of my petrified body and I began to shake, my friends noticed this and asked me what was the problem. I couldn't speak, I just pointed with a trembling finger at the seat opposite, for there sitting with a group of Helensburgh boys was the Psycho Killer from Hell himself, the grotesque twisted face which had been centimetres from mine on that dreadful night two weeks before, was now replaced with a happy ,semi-normal face. He was laughing and joking with his friends when suddenly he caught my eye.

Oh no!! ...please god no!!.... Surely I couldn't be so lucky as to escape death twice. Should I run and hide under a seat?... Should I get off the train at the next station?... Should I pull the emergency cord?... Surely he will recognise me and he will contort his face into that familiar, crazed look that is etched in my memory forever and he will produce the multi notched weapon of mass destruction from his inside pocket and finish the job he started a couple of weeks before. He was having a quiet, whispered conversation with his group of friends which I was convinced was hatching some devious plan to murder me, throw my bloodied body out of the train onto the tracks and say I fell or jumped. This second option I was now seriously considering, surely a quick death in front of a speeding train would be preferable to the certain, slow, painful death by knife which I was convinced he was plotting and was now undoubtedly my fate.

He got up slowly…, oh fuck, he was coming over to me…oh fuck…he put out his hand, it was empty,…it wasn't holding the instrument of my death, he indicated, with a nod of his head for me to put my trembling, sweaty hand in his…,I did….,he shook it.

"Hey, son…dye remember me?"

Remember him??...remember him??...stupid question... His face has been etched into my memory day and night, every second since two weeks ago….

"Yyyes…I rem m m member you in the Maryland".

Aye …well some of "THE BOYS" in my town in Helensburgh tell me you're alright and you're a friend of "THE BOYS."

Well whoever these *"BOYS "*were I was eternally grateful that they had given me such a glowing reference….

"Aye that's right I hang about with a llllot of Helensburgh boys on our ssssscooters."

He put his hand into his inside pocket and produced a half bottle of whisky, stuck out the bottle to me.Was this the same hand that held the knife to my throat which was now offering me a drink of his whisky?.....YES by god it really was…..

"Huv a wee drink with me and my boys here "

"Th Th Thanks a lot."

"Where are you boys going?"

"Were going to the Maryland club…and yyyyou?"

"Aye us too….listen son,"……

He put his face up to mine and with whisky breath, he winked and said….

"I'm sorry son about the other week…I've been told by my boys that it was a case of mistaken identity."

"If anybody ever gives you any bother you just tell them that you're a friend of mine and if they touch you then they'll huv to deal with me. Your boys and you will be fine, awright?"

"Aye fine….th... th... thanks a lot"

And so we became acquaintances, often meeting on the train to Glasgow or coming back. Or nodding to each other in the Maryland club while he was on the prowl for another victim.

It transpired that this Psycho Killer was called Mick McGuire or "Mental Mick" as he was known and was indeed the leader of the Helensburgh gang known as the "Beach Boys" and that mentioning his name was my passport to visit the pubs in Helensburgh anytime without ever being worried about attacks from local gangs...........

"Ye see that big lanky, mod, beanpole over there?"

"Aye that big freak o nature with the stupid haircut and the sticky oot ears"

"Aye him"

"Well he's from Dumbarton let's get him outside and chib him"

"NoNoNo!...ye canny touch him....he's a friend of Mental Mick"

"Whit that gleakit big eejit.....How can he be a friend o Mental Mick?"

"I don't know but "The Boys "say that if ye touch him ye'll huv Mental Mick to deal with"

"Ohhh fuck that...leave him alone then eh?"...let's pick another one"

The Two Rivers and Doon the Shore.

Oh the River Clyde, The wonderful Clyde

The name of it thrills me and fills me with pride

And I'm satisfied whate'er may betide

The sweetest of songs, is the song of The Clyde.

Dumbarton, the town of my birth and childhood lies at the mouth of two rivers , the River Clyde and the River Leven. The two rivers meet at the point where stands the historic Dumbarton Castle.

The most famous by far is the Clyde. Here along the banks were once the world famous bustling shipyards of Greenock, Dumbarton, Clydebank, Scotstoun, Whiteinch and Govan. Here in the glory days of the 40's, 50's and early 60's the craftsmen fashioned with their bare hands the most famous ships in the world. At the start of the 20th century a fifth of all the ships in the world were built on the Clyde almost 30.000 in total. The access to all local raw materials steel, wood etc.is one reason why the shipyards boomed and employed tens of thousands of highly skilled craftsmen. "Clyde built" became a benchmark of quality and excellence throughout the world and so contracts were awarded to the yards to build not only ocean going liners such as the Queen Mary and the Queen Elizabeth 2nd but also warships for the royal navy. These were the heady days of the shipbuilding industry, Where proud men toiled in poor conditions to complete orders then watch with puffy chests, glowing hearts and although they would never admit it, a tear in their eye, the product of months and sometimes years of hard graft being launched by royalty before preparing their yard to begin the labour of love all over again. The order books were full and the workers were able to plan their future with confidence and certainty. The communities of the shipyard towns along the banks of the Clyde grew and prospered. These were the glory days of the Clyde, now sadly gone For many years after the yards remained complete with their cranes long after they closed, as silent ghosts and sad reminders of The Clyde's and particularly Dumbarton's long and proud tradition of shipbuilding. Countries like Japan, China and Korea were able to produce ships at a cheaper price so nowadays only a few small specialist yards continue building yachts for the rich and famous and repair yards and breakers yards now exist in some of the towns.

My father was one of these skilled men, he was employed by Denny's shipyard as a hole borer, and when I was a child he always told me that he was a specialist because he was the only man in the world who could bore SQUARE holes, this piece of information I took great pride in telling all my school friends,

"My dad's better than your dad....he bores square holes in ships."

This boast was always met with howls of laughter instead of the undying admiration of my friends which I expected. It came as a huge disappointment when I discovered later that my dad was joking and that he only bored ordinary, round holes like everyone else.

While Denny's provided employment for the majority of the population of Dumbarton until it closed in 1964 it was Ballantine's Whisky distillery and the Justerini and Brooks bonded whisky warehouse which came to the rescue. With these two employers and all the related small local businesses most families had someone who worked in either the distillery or the bond this also gave the town the lovely daily smell of hops and grain being prepared for the distillation process of Ballantine's whisky, although the workers carried this distinct smell on their clothes and hair and into their houses. I always remember the smell when my Auntie Annie and Aunt Marie came home from work. The distillery workers also had the advantage of the perk of a glass of whisky every day after their shift or if they preferred they could save the shots until the end of the week and claim a bottle, a privilege which many seriously abused by quickly becoming alcoholics.

So this great river which flowed from the Lowther Hills, through Glasgow then widened when it reached Greenock on the Firth of Clyde then eventually flowed west and into the Atlantic was the lifeblood of the towns and cities on its banks and brought a new post war prosperity and confidence to the towns it touched.

My childhood was spent around this river, this is where we happily played as children, jumping the huge waves created by the enormous ships which sailed past our house in Brucehill on the way to unload their cargo in the Broomielaw docks in Glasgow. These ships were a constant source of fascination for me. When the tide was out the channel on the route to Glasgow was extremely narrow and if I walked out to the edge of the water I could almost touch the monstrous ships as they sailed past within what seemed like arms reach. The noise of their engines was deafening and the shore shook with the vibration looking up on the decks I could wave and shout to the crew who often waved and shouted back to me, mostly in foreign languages which I couldn't understand. After they had past I would just stand and stare at the rear of the ship with the names and their home port on the stern I was enthralled by these mysterious, unknown and unpronounceable places which I had never heard of in my life…….. Cancun, Malaysia, Copenhagen, Amsterdam, Hamburg etc. Where were these places? Who lives there? What do they look like? So many questions I needed answered. Asking my parents was a waste of time I just got the same answer…

"Where's Malaysia mammy?"

"Ach don't know son…where did ye leave it?"

"No mammy, Malaysia is a country somewhere, I saw the name on the back of a big ship that just sailed past.

"Whit? Achh away and ask yer teacher, and don't be askin me daft questions while I'm busy making the tea"

So I did…..

My geography teacher was Mrs Dennett, a small portly, middle aged woman with a shiny, round red face and a wild mop of red curly hair, one of my favourite teachers, she wore traditional teacher's half circle glasses perched on the end of her nose so she could look down to read and look up to see normally so her eyes always dancing up and down like a fruit machine while she was explaining points of geography to us. She always took time to answer my many questions about far off distant countries. She was more than happy that I was taking such an interest in geography and she showed me on the maps exactly where these places were. This was a revelation to me to discover that outside of my wee town of Dumbarton was another huge world and moreover most parts of that world could be reached by boat. I loved geography and excelled in the subject, devouring every piece of information, listening intently to Mrs Dennett's explanations and searching on maps for places I had never heard of and had no idea existed.

One Christmas I asked my parents for a world atlas and an I-spy book of ships.

"Whit? Dae ye no want toys or a selection box then."

"No mammy I want to learn about the world and stuff"

"Achh away oot an play an don't be so daft …..Wait and see whit Santa brings ye"

So armed with my maps and my books of ships from Santa, I embarked on my mission of discovery. My Grannies house in Brucehill was my main observation post as it overlooked the stretch of the Clyde from Gourock to port Glasgow and I would spend all my time sitting there at the big window in the living room watching the ships passing then looking them up in my books to identify the type of vessel and then searching in my world atlas for the home port and then plot the thousands of miles across the seas they had taken to the point where they had to pass my grannies living room window. My imagination ran wild with the images of their long voyage across the vast oceans of the world.

Oh how I longed to be on one of these ships.

The channel up the Clyde was very narrow and dangerous and only some smaller ships could navigate it safely, of course the ships had to sail very slowly and be guided by tugs to avoid running aground. These tugs were pilot tugs which would sail down to the mouth of the Clyde at Greenock to meet the ship and then guide it slowly up the narrow, dangerous channel of the Clyde to unload their cargos at Glasgow docks in the Broomielaw…So I became an expert at recognising when a big ship was due to pass by watching for the tugs passing on the way to Greenock to collect the ship. This was my signal to grab my bike and quickly race down to the shore in time to witness the spectacle of these enormous ships being towed or guided back to Glasgow close up. The thrill I felt as I stood within touching distance of these monsters was indescribable, shouting hello and waving to the crew and them shouting and waving back were some of the most memorable moments of my childhood.

I'm positive that this childhood hobby gave me an interest in world travel and a fascination and love of boats which I still have to this day.

Of course the Clyde was not just a working river, there were many pleasure boats which used the Clyde as a gateway to other waters around the west coast of Scotland and beyond. One of the summer highlights for our family was the annual outing to the Iles of Bute, we would sail on the paddle steamers like the Jeannie Deans or the Waverly which took families in summer from the Broomilaw in Glasgow to Craigendoran, Dunnoon and Rothsay.The sailings only took place during the summer and when my parents announced that next weekend we would be going on one of these day trips I couldn't sleep for days before because of my excitement and would annoy my parents by asking a million questions about the forthcoming excursion……

"What time will we leave?"

"What time will we arrive in Rothsay?"

"What is the name of the steamer we're going on?"

"Can I go to the engine room? Can I go on deck? OH. Please mammy, please!!"

We would travel by train to Glasgow early in the morning by train from Dumbarton Central and board the steamer in the docks at the Broomielaw. Sometimes the steamers called in at Craigendoran, near Helensburgh so we could catch the blue train to Helensburgh and get off at Craigendoran Pier. These steamers were for me an opportunity to fulfil my fantasies. I would run around the ship excitedly pretending to be the captain then go to the engine room where there was a viewing area where you could watch as the huge engines worked to power the paddles which drove the ship through the water, this for me was incredible and I would just stand and stare in awe of the enormous power and noise and revel in the heady smell of oil and diesel fuel. There was also a viewing window for the huge paddles as big as houses and I would be mesmerised for ages just watching as they powered the ship through the water churning up the foaming, murky waters of the Clyde. Of course as we passed Dumbarton I was out on deck looking down at the very spot where I often stood to watch the ships pass then strain my eyes as we sailed past Brucehill to pick out my grannies house and the big window where I sat for many hours with my atlas and my I-Spy books. My fantasy was that I was one of the crew of one of the cargo ships on route to a far off foreign port such as Cancun or Aruba and would wave enthusiastically to anyone on the shore just like the sailors did to me.We would spend the day in Rothesay playing on the beach and eating fish and chips but for me the thrill of the sailing was the best part of the day and I couldn't wait to repeat the adventure later by sailing back to Glasgow on the evening tide.

The Clyde wasn't only a working river, it also was the focus of our summer fun. Usually sometime during July the sun would be shining in a clear blue sky, the summer haze shrouding the Port Glasgow hills and distant mountains, adults would be sitting outside their houses on the doorsteps drinking tea and us kids would be digging the wee stone chips out of the melting tarmac with a lollipop stick and waiting impatiently for Palombo's ice cream van to appear so we could quench our thirst with an ice cream cone and a bottle of Irn Bru .With the pungent aroma of burning grass and wood smoke hanging heavily in the air and the temperature a scorching 18 or 20 degrees, these were the signals that today was a "doon the shore " day. One of the special days of the summer when entire families from all over Dumbarton would head "doon the shore" to spend the whole day relaxing, playing, eating and drinking beer in the sunshine.

The men wearing their vests and with their trouser legs rolled up to their knees and the women with their flowery summer frocks and stockings rolled down to their ankles.

All my uncles and aunts and cousins arrived early in the morning so me ,my sister and all our cousins were issued with instructions and sent off to scour the shore and secure the best places before the crowds started arriving at the bus terminus in Bontine Avenue and forming a long line marching like an army of ants heading down past Firth View Terrace and onwards to the stairs next to the cliff which led down to the shoreline, carrying all their provisions and equipment prepared to spend a day " Doon the shore."

"Noo away ye all go…and make sure you get the best places afore all them buggers fae Bellsmyre arrive"... said my Mum.

"Aye yer right there May "...replied my Grannie... *"It´s our shore and they all come here once or twice a year and steal aw the best places"*

"Noo skedaddle and run as fast as yer wee legs will take ye."

The adults busied themselves by peeling the potatoes and preparing the vegetables for the dinner which would then be transported in huge pots before being cooked on an open fire of old bits of driftwood which littered the banks of the Clyde. This task of securing the best spot we always carried out enthusiastically, choosing carefully a big enough space for our large family, carefully cleaning away any broken glass, stones and general debris washed ashore by the tide, and trying not to be too close to other families, which of course was virtually impossible as it seemed that whole population of Dumbarton had the same idea as us. The shore extended from Levengrove Park to the Scottish Rocks, that's around 4 miles of available space, however the section between Brucehill and Westcliffe, commonly known as Havoc was the closest to the two main entrance paths so these spots were the most sought after and on days like this were like gold dust. So us kids headed off to the shore, running excitedly to the cliff, not for us the easy access stairs which went from Firth View past the Kiel school and to the shore. The easy route was for adults, we preferred the excitement of sliding down the cliff face.

The cliff was exactly that, a red sandstone cliff eroded through the years into a 45 degree, red, sandy surface covering volcanic rock upon which Brucehill was built. The cliff was our childhood playground we knew every path and bush and rock on its face. From the top we could slide straight down on any old piece of wood you could find lying around or if not then just sit on your hunches and let go, soon you were flying through the air at a hectic pace and tearing the arse out of your trousers at the same time ripping the skin off your knees and arms ,this always guaranteed a good slap on the legs from my mum but with the thrill and excitement of the moment any punishment was well worth it. My mum was continually sewing patches on the arse of my trousers, and many a good slap I got too.......

"What have I told ye about sliding doon the cliff on yer backside eh...slap...eh?" slappity slap slap.

"I couldn't help it mammy...I fell."

"Fell??? ....I'll gie ye fell"....."Dae ye think I´ve nothing better to dae than keep sewing new backsides on yer troosers.... ya wee tinker."*...slappity, slappity slap slap

When we arrived at the shore we would scour the shoreline and choose what we thought was the best place for our families. Later the rest of the relatives and friends would arrive heavily laden with all the equipment including, cans of beer, usually Tennents lager, the obligatory bottle of Ballantine's whisky, pots and pans to cook the Sunday lunch, the kettle and the teapot of course.. A tent would be erected as a changing room and as shade from the sun and us kids despatched on a mission to collect wood to start a fire in order to cook the potatoes and vegetables.

"Noo mind we don't want any wet wood...it won't burn...we need dry bits of stick tae get the fire going."

"Noo away ye go and bring it back quick....we want to start the dinner."

The adults would spend their time talking and cooking the dinner and drinking the beer and whisky, while we children were free to do whatever we wanted until we were called when the lunch was ready. The air became heavy with the lovely smells of wood smoke and boiling potatoes. This shoreline was for us another adventure playground.

If the tide was in we could swim in the brown, murky, oily river and if it was out we played in the smelly mud and silt, often fashioning makeshift boats out of logs or lumps of wood which were deposited on the shore by the ships, jumping into the water or rolling around in the mud and having mud fights were the innocent childhood games we played.

We didn't know or care how filthy it was, we had never heard of pollution or germs in those days. Of course the highlight was when a big cargo ship came into sight. A cry would go out that one was coming so everyone raced to the edge of the water pushing and jostling each other to get the best position to wait for the waves. What fun we had trying to jump the huge waves and getting covered in the stinking, sticky mud.

There was a long concrete pipe about 3 feet in diameter and about 20 yards long which came from the bank and stuck out into the river. This we used as a diving board, when the tide was in we would run along the length of this pipe as fast as possible then dive or jump into the water at the end, when the tide was out we would play a game to see who could crawl the furthest through the mud inside the pipe, little did we know then that this was actually a sewage pipe and what we were diving into and crawling through was raw sewage.

When the tide came in it entered into the pipe and collected the sewage dragging it out into the Clyde where it floated around until the tide took it away and into the channel then later into the Atlantic. But what fun we innocently had, not so much swimming as going through the motions, until we were called in by our parents to have a jam sandwich which of course we devoured hungrily, licking our fingers so as not to lose any of the flavour.

Of course we had to pack up all out belongings and leave the shore before dusk, because that was when the midges arrived to feast on the blood of the day-trippers. Midges are small mosquitoes which turn the sky dark when they arrive to attack in packs.

 Where I live now in Spain we have a lot of mosquitoes, however these Spanish mosquitoes are total amateurs compared to their Scottish counterparts. Here they give you a polite, almost apologetic little nip and sip a smidgen of blood then fly away. Not for Scottish midges this mamby pamby courteous method...Ohhh Nooo....Scottish midges land on your skin and drill through it like a woodpecker cutting into a tree, they go through skin, sinew and bone until the reach their target.....your veins....and then drink at least a pint of your blood whilst looking you straight in your eye with an evil death stare just daring you to try to swat them. When one has filled its stomach with enough of your blood to last a week he somehow silently, signals to all his friends and family that your blood is sweet and contains all the ingredients that constitute a banquet including alcohol, then they all arrive to drink their fill too. If you think you can escape by simply running away from them ...think again... These midges are expert trackers, once they have the smell of your blood they will follow you home and when finally you think you are safe inside your house they will come in through the tinniest of gaps in the doors and windows, find you, and continue their onslaught while you sleep.

So at 6.0 clock before the killer midges arrived we left the shore and trudged back up the cliff to home. We would arrive home tired but happy and after spending all day playing in the sun we would be as red as tomatoes. This was the time for the most torturous and least enjoyable part of the day. My mum made me and my sister lie on the bed belly down while she covered us with her special, favourite sunburn remedy...sour milk....

In summer a couple of bottles were always left all day in the sun on the window ledge in our kitchen to help them to ferment and become sour, when this horrible, smelly potion was applied liberally the smell was enough to knock out a horse and our house stank of this vile lotion, not to mention our beds constantly smelled of sour milk. Thinking about this old wives tale now it seems barbaric, but then we were Scottish children of the sixties and finding a shop which sold sun cream in Scotland was impossible.

There wasn't a shopkeeper in Scotland who was willing to invest money in a complete box of sun cream and only sell one bottle a year.

Whilst our part of the Clyde in Dumbarton served as our summer playground, the real jewel in the crown was the town of Helensburgh. Helensburgh, for us, was the real seaside. An elegant Georgian town, the birthplace of John Logie Baird, the inventor of television, Henry Bell the engineer who pioneered steam travel and of course where our own modern day hero Jackie Stewart, world champion racing driver lived. It even had a clean, pebble beach, complete with donkey rides, Punch and Judy shows and ice cream shops and of course an open air swimming pool. Now, at this point, I have to remind you that my country Scotland in summer is not exactly the Bahamas. The summer temperature if you're lucky can be as high as 20 degrees or as low as...well freezing.

If there is three hours of unbroken sunshine with a temperature of 20 degrees in one day it constitutes a heat wave and will forever after be referred to as the long hot summer of that particular year and will be the topic of conversation for months in the streets and pubs around Dumbarton….

"Oh my god it was toooooo hot, I needed to go intae ma hoose away from the scorching sun…ah canny staun this heat."

So you can imagine that in a country with such a diverse climate swimming in an open air, unheated swimming pool would not be classed as one of life's greatest pleasures, but, for me and my sister it was a big part of our summer trips to Helensburgh and was obligatory for us children to swim in it, funnily enough in all my childhood trips to this pool I can never remember seeing any adults swimming in it. After coming out of the pool with our pale blue lips and feeling so numb with the cold that we were trembling, and with chattering teeth and knocking knees, what better treat than a lovely ice cream, followed by a donkey ride? This to us really was luxury and when we finally thawed out we would be chattering excitedly about it for days, boasting to our friends about how many lengths we could swim underwater, then pestering our parents to take us there again.

My father had now left Denny's shipyard and was now working as a furniture delivery driver for Mason's furniture shop. Masons was a famous local furniture shop in the High Street in Dumbarton which at this time became very successful due to the new surge in social housing growth in Dumbarton. Families were now moving out of the old damp, crumbling houses and into nice new flats and houses in the housing estates of Brucehill, Castlehill, Westcliffe and Bellsmyre and in Masons they could buy all the furniture they needed for their nice new house "on tick".

As his job entailed delivering the furniture to all parts of Dunbartonshire he often had to go as far as Arrochar, Tarbet, and Balloch and in fact any part of the county. He would often surprise us on a Saturday with a trip in his van to Arrochar.

"Come on I´ve got some deliveries in Arrochar and Tarbet"

"I'll drop ye in Arrochar and then collect ye when I finish the deliveries"

"Get yer stuff and get in the back with the furniture"

We didn't need to be told twice .Me and my sister jumped excitedly into the back with the furniture while my mum had the luxury of sitting in the front cab with my dad and his van boy Jimmy Mcculloch.We loved these trips, the road to Arrochar ran along the banks of Loch Long and was a series of small hills. When the van flew over these hills it would bounce up in the air and me and my sister would scream with delight as we flew in the air, of course being in the back of a van with no windows in virtual darkness we never knew when a hill was coming so me and Marie Therese, my sister would stand with our arms out holding onto each other and revelling in the suspense and anticipation of the next one. She would goad me by continually telling me that a hill was coming now and letting me go so I was standing unsupported and nearly wetting myself with fear and anticipation. Of course the furniture was securely tied down so I don't think that there was ever really any danger of being crushed to death.

My mum packed all the equipment we needed for the day and my dad would drop us off in Arrochar then continue with his deliveries, returning later to spend some time with us and then repeat the bouncy van experience again on the way home.

Now if having the river Clyde as our playground wasn't enough we also had the River Leven.

This 7 mile stretch of water runs from Balloch at the mouth of Loch Lomond to Dumbarton, passing through the towns of Alexandria and Renton most commonly known as the Vale of Leven.The stretch which passes through Dumbarton is littered with small leisure boats, some well cared for and others sunken wrecks. At the intersection between the Clyde and the Leven lies Levengrove Park on one bank and the town centre on the other. The town centre bank or "doon the quay" as it was more popularly known was where the local drunks would gather to drink their Eldorado, sing songs like Flower of Scotland to the swans which always congregated there waiting for some old grannie to throw them some morsels of food and this is where the winos gathered for their daily intellectual political debates which usually ended with someone getting punched or even thrown into the river. This was quite a dangerous part of town for children as we were well warned by our parents not to go too near the edge as the raging currents of this fast flowing river would drag us under in seconds and would result in certain death by drowning and we would never reappear this was enough for us to keep away, but never stopped us goading each other to go nearer in our games of dare......

"Go on ya big fearty...go closer"

"No...No...no... I canny "...

"Scaredy scaredy custard yer face is made of mustard"

Then would begin a lot of pushing and shoving then running and chasing each other into the safety of Levengrove Park.

Of course there were disasters and stories were banded about of children as well as drunk winos drowning in this part of the river.

When my father was a van driver for Mason's furniture I clearly remember one such day.

Masons furniture shop was in Dumbarton high street however their furniture warehouse was on the quay next to the river. Here is where my father used to reverse his van up to the back doors of the store in order to load on the furniture which he had to deliver to the homes of the customers. During the school holidays he would often take me and my sister with him, we loved this, not least because we were allowed to travel in the back of the van and then help him to carry the small items of furniture into the customers houses, who would then reward us with sweets, apples or if we were really lucky small change. One day we were with my dad loading his van and me and my sister were busy playing chasing each other round the van and running to the edge of the quay and back again when suddenly we could hear a lot of shouting and screaming coming from near the edge of the quay.

"Help...help...help somebody help she's fell in...She's fell in.my wee lassie is in the river"

Looking across we could see a woman having hysterics and pointing into the river.

My dad appeared coming out of the warehouse carrying a chair to put into the van.

"Daddy...daddy...quick a wee lassie has fallen into the river".

My dad without a second's hesitation and with no regard for his own safety bounded towards the river and launched himself off the edge of the quay and started swimming towards the poor girl who was by now gaining speed and being carried away by the treacherous, fast flowing current.

My dad was a very strong swimmer and somehow swimming like an Olympic champion. He managed to grab hold of her and hold on to her. Meantime me and my sister were staring transfixed with my sister screaming and crying, thinking that my dad was surely going to drown himself in this futile rescue attempt.

He dragged the distressed girl to the side where by now a crowd had gathered and everyone helped him and the girl out of the water. He just walked calmly back to the warehouse saying he had to go home to get changed into some dry clothes to continue with his deliveries. And warned us that this is what happens when you get too close to the edge.

Later he received recognition in the form of a bravery award and medal from the mayor of Dumbarton. My dad typically played down his part in the life saving mission by saying that he wasn´t particularly brave and that if he had stopped to think then perhaps he wouldn't have dived in. Luckily for the girl my dad didn't hang back for a second to weigh up the situation.

So this dangerous river was another playground, although after this incident me and my sister never went near the edge of the quay ever again and would always be warning other kids who we saw too close to be careful. And recounting the story as a warning to them.

My favourite part of The Leven was the short stretch between Balloch and the mouth of Loch Lomond, this is where as a 13 year old I spent most of my weekends and school holidays helping my Uncle repairing and restoring his boat.

My uncle Harry Cochrane was my mum's cousin but I called him uncle. He and his English wife Gwen didn't have any children and so after finding out through my mum about my keen interest in boats he asked my mum if it would be O.K. for him to collect me on Saturday mornings and I could go and help him with the work on his boat in Balloch, I could sleep on his boat with him and Gwen and he would bring me back on Sunday night.

"Aye sure thing Harry. Sure the boy sits staring out of the window at every ship that passes up the Clyde."

"And he´s always got his heid buried in his books about ships"

These weekends for me were fantastic, My uncle Harry had been in the merchant navy for many years and had sailed all over the world, his stories kept me spellbound as he recounted his numerous adventures and experiences at sea, of course he had to suffer my endless questions about the countries he had visited and the things he had seen, meantime we were painting or varnishing the outside and inside of his boat. I think he was happy that he had someone with the same enthusiasm as him and we had a fantastic relationship. Gwen would cook dinner for us in the galley while we both kept busy with the repairs or we would take out the motorboat and two fishing rods and Uncle Harry taught me how to catch trout and even on occasion salmon, although this was illegal we would cover it with cloth and sail quickly back to the shore and Harry would give a friendly wave to the local river gamekeeper who was patrolling the river in his wee boat keeping a watchful eye out for salmon poachers..

"Oh shit it's the gilly"...said harry ....."Quick hide the salmon son".

My previous instructions from Uncle Harry rang in my ears.

"Noo mind "...he had said..."if we see the gamekeeper hold the salmon tight so it disnae jump about on the bottom of the boat...and make sure ye hide it under the cloth and put the trout on top so if the nosey wee bugger looks in he can only see the trout."

I quickly kicked it under my seat, covered it with a cloth and placed the still wriggling trout on top.

"Hello there Harry...how's it going....who's the wee boy?"

"AH ....hello there Jim...he's my wee nephew ...just showing him around the river and teaching him how to fish err ...err...for pike or trout.

"Aye well mind and teach him that he canny fish for salmon here...it´s illegal"

"Oh sure thing Jim...wouldn't dream of such a thing".

"Aye I know that Harry..... But there are some folk fishing for salmon illegally here and I widnae want the boy to think that it was ok".

"Sure thing Jim....these poachers should be shot Jim...nae trial ...nae judge.... just shot on sight ... eh?

"NO Harry then I widnae huv a job...hahahahahah."

So back to the boat we went laughing our heads off about our close shave and presenting our beautiful fresh salmon for Gwen to work her magic.

Uncle Harry had a cabin cruiser and a motorboat and during the summer he was also the skipper of a tourist boat which sailed from McAllister's boat yard and took tourists around the loch, stopping the engines at intervals and explaining all the places of interest. He told me one day that when I had school holidays I could be his boat boy. I started off as his assistant and soon he taught me how to sail the boat and later to give the commentaries to the tourists who always rewarded me at the end of the tour with generous tips. I became an expert on local history and would burry my head in books and study and learn all the relevant information about dates etc.

For me this was heaven and I would be so excited every Friday knowing that Uncle Harry would be collecting me in his M.G Magnette the following morning for my weekend of adventure. Uncle harry taught me everything about sailing boats, how the engines worked, how to sail without engines using wind power, navigating by the sun, moon and stars how to forecast weather conditions. Tidal movements, currents...etc. these were life skills which I never learned at school and which have helped me many times in my life.

Unfortunately my Uncle Harry moved to live in England and took his boat with him so ended my maritime education.

I missed him a lot and will always remember and be grateful for the adventures we had together and the time I spent on the Leven and on Loch Lomond and all the fun I had with my dear Uncle Harry and Aunt Gwen.

The River Leven as it flows through Dumbarton is fast flowing and with treacherous rip tides. We were well aware of the dangers but still as adventurous, fearless boys we used to pass many hours playing in and around it.It was littered with old abandoned boats and was full of trout and salmon.

My best friend was John White and me were both keen on fishing. Some Saturdays we would get up really early and catch a bus to Helensburgh then another to Garelochhead where we spent the day happily fishing for pike or cod until the sun disappeared then trudge back to the top of the hill to catch the last bus back to Helensburgh then back to Dumbarton, usually with one or two pike or cod to show for our day out and for our mums to cook for dinner.

Now and again we would also go fishing on the River Leven. You needed to buy a day licence each time which gave you permission or run the risk of being caught by the water ranger known as "the gilly".

One sunny day we decided to go fishing in the afternoon after school for an hour or so. We figured that as the chances of being caught in such a short time was minimal we would forego the obligatory licence and take the risk by keeping a watchful eye on the river for any sign of the gilly.

All was going well and we had landed a couple of nice rainbow trout. The bigger fish were surfacing and catching flies further out in the middle of the river and so we decided to wade out to the middle where there was a small island with a tree in the middle. In our excitement and enthusiasm we unfortunately overlooked the fact that the tide was coming in and by the time we realized our mistake it was already too late and the rising water was lapping around our ankles, we were now stranded on an ever shrinking island in the middle of the fast flowing river .With our retreat to dry land now cut off the only remedy, we decided, was to climb the tree. So grabbing our fishing gear and the couple of trout we climbed the tree, sat on the branches and shouted for help. On a normal day there were usually some small boats passing along this stretch and other fishermen around on the banks. But today just when we needed help no-one appeared. It was late afternoon and starting to get dusk and we were beginning to get really worried and envisaged staying on these tree branches until the tide went out again the following morning. Finally, after what seemed like hours we heard the welcome sound of an outboard engine and a small boat appeared containing the figure of a man. We were ecstatic and began waving and shouting for help. Unfortunately for us it was the gilly

He spotted us and came closer…...

"What are you two daft eedjits doing up that tree,"

"Err... well we were fishing and the tide came in then we couldn't get back."

"Wait a minute then I'll come over and pick you up and take you to the bank."

OH shit…….. We just remembered we were fishing illegally with no day permit AND we had two trout in our hands.

Me and John gave each other a knowing look, swallowed hard and shouted back…….

"No, No….don't worry we'll be alright here till the tide goes out. We're fine thanks. We've got a flask of tea and some sandwiches…..no bother."

"Whit dae ye mean yer fine ...the tide won't go out for another 12 hours and it will be dark soon, ye canny sit on that tree all night."

"Climb down and get in the boat."

So down we climbed into the boat leaving the two trout on the branch of the tree well out of sight of the gilly.

He rowed us to the opposite bank with a lecture about observing tide times and helped us out with our fishing gear.

"Now let that be a lesson to you two eedjits next time yer fishing here make sure you know the times of the tides."

"OH …..And next time be sure to buy a fucking licence."

Of course the tide had risen more and was now almost touching the branches of the tree we had previously been sitting on.

We watched him sailing back to the tree, reaching up to the branch where we had been sitting and collecting our trout...with a cheery wave and a sly smirk he was off down the river with our two trout for his tea.

At the junction where the two great rivers meet lies Levengrove Park...The jewel in the crown of Dumbarton is located on a dramatic stretch of land where the River Leven meets the estuary of the River Clyde. With extensive panoramic views across the Clyde to Renfrewshire, across the Leven to the town centre and the quay and Dumbarton Rock on the other side of the Leven.This Park played a major role in my childhood. It served as an adventure playground where we were free to run around safely, play putting on summer evenings, 20 a side Sunday football and illegal cycle track where we cycled as fast as possible around the tracks keeping a careful look out for the parkie.It was our shortcut from the town centre along the shore to Brucehill, and a meeting place for teenage boys and girls where you could disappear into the bushes or behind trees for a bit of snogging or if you were lucky some touchy feely. In the summer it had Palombo's ice cream parlour where we could gather together and slurp our ice creams mixed with American cream soda to make a cool, satisfying frothy drink. There was also a paddling pool which filled up with the murky water of the Clyde when the tide came in and you could have a paddle in the summer as long as you kept your shoes on as it was always full of broken glass.

The Sunday football matches here were legendary and took place in the Posties...a special area marked out for football and with proper goalposts. The match started after lunch and would carry on until dark or when the owner of the ball had to go home for his dinner. There would be at least 20 on each side and with no referee the matches often had to stop for ten minutes or more while two opponents rolled around on the floor punching and kicking each other over an offside dispute. I was never that keen on football, mainly because it was a well-known fact that, with two left feet I couldn't kick a ball to save my life, but I enjoyed the camaraderie and would present myself for selection by the team captains who sometimes ended up fighting because none of them wanted me on their side and then tossing a coin with the loser forced to have me in their team......

"OH no...It's heids...make it the best of three eh???"

"No, no...We agreed the loser gets skinny malinky longlegs."

"Ach ok...ok....right big yin you're in my team...but stay back and try to kick the ball when it lands at yer feet instead of turning yer back, tripping over yer big feet or runnin away in the opposite direction...ya big Jessie......"

The games were a chaotic shambles with a distinct lack of rules meaning anyone and everyone could chase the ball, no one had any particular playing position so this would result in 20 boys chasing the same ball and being tackled by 20 other players .There were no goalkeepers and no defenders everybody was an attacking forward. Injured players simply limped off the pitch wincing in pain, collected their jackets and stumbled off home. Some players arrived in full kit in the colours of their favourite team and there were always fights with a player in Celtic colours playing in the same team as a boy in Rangers colours. The game would descend into chaos while these two, despite playing for the same side, tackled each other for possession of the ball with the kicks continuing long after the ball was at the feet of another player. These Sunday afternoon matches always attracted a crowd of spectators, mostly teenage girls who hadn't any interest in football but merely came to giggle, flirt and shout for their favourite player, who would then puff out his chest and put on a spectacular display of fancy footwork often launching a well-aimed ball at the crowd of girls, later after the game in Palombo's cafe he would be trying to chat up the same girls who a short time before he was trying to break their bones. Anyone bothering to keep track of the score would shout out

"It's 43-27----so let's make it next goal wins eh boys........it's getting dark."

So the game would end and everyone would wander off home for tea.

Primary School

I remember clearly my first day at primary school, over the years some memories fade into the distance but my first day at West Bridgend Primary School in, Dalreoch, and Dumbarton is etched permanently in my memory.

I was five years old and my mum had taken out a Provident cheque and had gone to the Co-operative shop in the High street and bought me the full school uniform. Green blazer with a St Patrick's shield which she had hand sewn onto the top pocket, "Tradamus Lampada" was the motto, in Latin, above the shield which was a castle with a cross above... I, of course, had not the remotest idea what this meant, later at secondary school I took Latin and discovered that it meant "holding the torch". She bought me short, heavy woollen, grey trousers, I was only allowed to wear long trousers when I went to the "big school", held up by a green and gold belt with a snake buckle, A white shirt and a green and grey and yellow striped tie and a green v neck jersey, grey, long socks with green and yellow stripes round the top, black shoes and of course a wee green cap again with the same wee shield on the front. Each item of clothing of course with a wee label sewn on by my mum, with my name written on it...I was very proud to be going to school and looked in the big mirror in my mum's bedroom at my reflection.

My mum took out a hanky, licked the corner and wiped my face.......

"Ahhhh son you look smashing."

"My wee boy is growing up so fast."...said my mum with a wee tear in her eye.

Of course we then had to walk to Brucehill first to visit my grannie Gow to show her how "smashing" I looked.

"OH my god, look at ye...sure you look such a big boy."....gushed my grannie spitting on her hand and smoothing my hair.

"Now here's a wee present for ye, put it in yer pocket and save it for later."

My hopes of it being a bar of five boys chocolate quickly faded as I watched her put a neatly folded, white cotton hanky into my top pocket.....

"It's got yer initials on it so that if ye lose it then whoever finds it will know whose it is."

She obviously forgot, in her excitement that the school would be full of other wee boys with the initial "J"

Maybe she thought that it could be recognised by the contents of green snot which would be distinctly mine.

So off we went with me reluctantly holding my mums hand for the 10 minute walk down Brucehill to West Bridgend, joining on the way the rest of the wee boys and mums from the estate the same age as me and all starting the same school together. On the way the mums were all chattering excitedly together about their worries and how nervous and proud they were of their wee boys first day at school whilst we were made to walk next to them in case we dirtied our nice new uniforms.

"Now don't you be running away and falling and skinning yer knees, ya wee tinker!"

"No mammy."

"And don't scuff them new shoes, and don't be playing fitba at playtime!"

"No mammy."

"Be polite to the teachers, if they talk to you you have to say …yes miss…no miss."

"Aye mammy."

"An don't you dare show me up ya wee rascal."

"Yes mammy….I mean no mammy."

"And I'll be waitin at the gate at dinner time to take ye home for dinner then ye can come back again in the afternoon."

"And remember to use that hanky that your grannie gave ye if your nose is running. Don't you dare be in your class with them snotters of yours dangling off the end of yer nose and giving me a right showing up."

"Aye right mammy."

On the way we passed by big St Pats which was the secondary school where in a few short years we would all be attending. As we passed St Michaels church we all had to salute and make the sign of the cross on our foreheads as a mark of respect and to show the world what good wee catholic boys we were. Failure to remember this ritual would result in a hard slap on the legs or the back of the head accompanied with the stern warning that if I forgot again god would punish me and I would surely go straight to hell for all eternity. I didn't fancy the idea of burning in hell…I was used to heating my hands and freezing cold backside in front of our coal fire and knew that if I stood too long my bare legs would look like corned beef and my hands would be stinging with the heat of the fire…and that was only for 5 minutes so I was certain that this eternity would be quite a bit longer. So I imagined that doing this for *ALL* eternity would be rather painful…so I saluted and crossed my forehead dutifully.

Outside the school all the mums were fussing and crying and wee scared, shy boys were holding tight to their mums hand or burying their faces in her coat and scared to death of the forthcoming event…..

"Maaammy ah don't want tea go in…I want to stay with you! "

"Mammy am scared!"

"Mammy, why do I have to go to school?"…"bwaaahaaa!!"

"Ahh c'mon son, sure you'll be fine once ye get in…The teachers are lovely and before ye know it it'll be home time."

"Noo away ye go. Let go of my coat and be a brave wee soldier."

"Whhaaaaaa!!!….mmmaaaaammmyyy!!!"

Of course we had all been told about the school and the lovely teachers who would look after us just like our mums and offered bribes of sweeties on the way to encourage us to enter into this scary, unknown place. It didn't help that the school building itself was ancient, dirty and dark and gloomy and looked more like a prison than a primary school. Built in the late 1800s it was previously a protestant school…any non-denominational school at that time was called a protestant school…so when it became uninhabitable, the previous pupils were moved out to a nice new school and the building was then bought by the catholic church and after a quick clean with a feather duster, put to use, with very few improvements, as a catholic primary school.

Although only 5 years old I already knew this word protestant which we shortened to "proddy".This was the word that adults used to describe anything and anybody not catholic.

There was no investigation and no debate...non-Catholic equalled protestant. We children used it, without knowing the meaning, in the streets to tease and taunt other children........

"Proddy...Proddy...you're a wee Proddy.".....

"No I'm not...no am not...I'm telling ma mammy on you"...

Then we would scatter in all directions in case the mammy came out and slapped us for calling her wee boy names.

I was continually being told that these proddies were our enemies and should be avoided at all costs. Of course I had no idea why, no detailed explanations were ever given...this was simply an undisputed fact of life.

"Noo Joseph you mustn't play with any of them protestant children at number 8 across the road."

"But mammy that's no fair the wee boy always has sweeties or chocolate and he always shares them with me....he's my pal."

"Do as you're told or I'll slap your legs."

Having experienced many times, so far in my young life my mammy's style of leg slapping which always left a red mark in the exact shape of her hand I reluctantly obeyed.

So today on my first day of school I was the odd one out, I couldn't wait to get in there and away from all these screaming and crying boys and the overprotective mums, I let go of my mums hand, said a quick *"cheerio mammy"* and I was off exploring my new surroundings and the huge playground and marvelling at the space around the building which surely was just waiting for me to have adventures and play my imaginary games. Although I was too young to take all this in I was nevertheless excited about the prospect of this new experience. With a quick wave my mum disappeared into the distance, while all the others waited in the playground until the bell rang and the teachers appeared. After a head count and a roll call the new children had to line up in pairs and hold hands with their partner. The teachers soon realized that one of the new boys was missing. Panic ensued and a search party of older boys were instructed to search the grounds.

"Well his name's on the list...look...Joseph Mcloughlin." said Miss Slorach, the head teacher.

*"Aye and I saw him with his mammy at the gate so I know he is here somewhere "*replied Mrs Connolly.

"Maybe his mammy took him back home"

"No because I saw his mammy May Gow walking back up the road by herself....so he must be here".

I was eventually discovered by the search party playing happily in the dirt behind the school building pretending to be a cowboy who was hiding from the Indian posse who were looking for me to take me prisoner and take my scalp. My new shiny uniform well and truly christened and with a few rips in the nice new trousers and scuff marks on my new shoes.

The teachers at West Bridgend Primary were indeed kind and helpful and I particularly was happy learning new skills such as reading, writing and counting all taught with a great deal of encouragement and kindness. Not for them the discipline we would encounter in the future at big school. We needed to learn the basic skills, "The Three R's" and I loved every minute of it. The head teacher was Miss Slorach,I found out later that her full name was Fanny Slorach,of course in my naive childhood I had never heard of, let alone used sexual innuendo ,only when I was older did I realize all the opportunities I had missed as an innocent child to make fun of her name. She was a lovely, kind lady who was probably in her thirties or forties but to us children she was ancient. Other teachers I remember were Mrs Mccallion, Mrs Connolly, and Miss White. And my favourite, Mrs McGuire..........

Mrs McGuire sat in the fire,

The fire was too hot she sat in the pot,

The pot was too hot, she sat in the Clyde

An all the wee fishes swam up her backside.

We used to chant in the playground, well out of earshot of Mrs McGuire

We spent our days playing games, singing and learning mathematics by using an abacus which taught us addition, subtraction and multiplication, we learned the times tables by memory with Mrs McGuire marching up and down the space between our desks bashing out the rhythm of the tables on each desk with a wooden ruler, we had regular times tables tests where she would stand at the front of the class and shout your name at random.......

"Joseph ......say the 8 times table"....

"Errrmmmm....8 ones 8"

"8 twos sixteen"

"8 threes 24"

"8 fours 32"

"Good...correct"

"Michael. Continue".....

This ritual was repeated with monotonous regularity until we could recite parrot fashion every table.

This method of teaching was such a successful life skill that I can still remember and use these tables to this day.

Writing consisted of copying words and sentences that the teacher had written with white chalk on the big blackboard.

With my tongue stuck out, saliva running down my chin and with immense concentration I learned how to write my name.

It wasn't until we were 7 or 8 years old that we learned "joined up writing."

Reading was from colourful books with lots of pictures of two children called Janet and John who were always happy and had fantastic adventures. Each sentence began with huge letters and I would use my little skinny fingers to follow the letters and words as I read them aloud and learned how to pronounce the sounds of the words.

I loved this new exciting skill and developed a love of reading which has never left me.

Of course we had P.E. too which everyone loved, this gave us children a chance to release all our excess energy by throwing bean bags at each other and playing football with soft balls in the gymnasium then in the playground it was physical exercises, wearing our white vests, white shorts and grey socks with black plimsolls we enjoyed running round in circles, running backwards, hopping on one leg, jumping as high as we could and of course playing football.

I was the tall skinny boy and as I was useless at kicking a ball always found myself being chosen as the goalkeeper with screams of laughter and ridicule as I hid my face with my hands every time someone kicked the ball in my direction with the ball going straight past me into the goal.

We had free milk which we drank through straws and enjoyed making slurping noises when the bottle was empty and the straw was only drawing air. This annoyed the teachers who would then choose two boys to go around with the crate and collect the empty bottles and take them to the janitor's room.

We had playtimes where we were free to run around outside for 15 minutes .Playing cowboys and Indians, was my favourite, I would ride my imaginary horse around the playground, slapping my own bum and making clicking sounds with my tongue I galloped around the playground pretending to be John Wayne or The Lone Ranger who I watched and cheered and booed every Saturday morning at the minors in the Rialto cinema. We played tag, Hide and Seek, or just chased each other around until we either caught our victim or simply got fed up and stopped.

Being an all-boys school, of course, there were often fights which would always draw an appreciative crowd of cheering spectators with small peripheral fights breaking out between the opposing supporters of whoever was fighting. The fights always continued for 5 minutes or so until a teacher came out of the staff room and grabbed the two opponents by the collar and marched them inside with a lecture about the rights and wrongs of fighting in the playground and a threat to report the offenders to their parents.

Shake hands and be friends and 2 minutes later all was back to normal again.

Of course as a catholic school we had the obligatory religious education lessons and prayers had to be learned by heart and said regularly. In every classroom there was a crucifix above the blackboard and statues of the Virgin Mary in the corner. Before and after each lesson we had to stand and face the crucifix for prayers the biggest preparations were saved for the momentous occasions when we would receive a visit from the priest. We were all warned in our assembly the day before he was due to arrive and were told to be on our best behaviour and that we should remember to be polite and salute the priest and if we should be lucky enough to be chosen to be spoken to or to be asked any questions always address him as "father". He would ask for a particular boy to say for example the "our father" or the "hail marry" and you would need to stand in front of the class and repeat the prayer with the eyes of all the teachers fixed on you and with them mouthing the words in case you should forget or make any mistakes and show up the school. He would end the assembly by telling us all to be good wee catholic boys and to respect our teachers, parents, priests, and in fact anyone who was older than us. Now this last bit of advice caused my wee mind some confusion as I knew of course that we should always be polite and respect teachers, parents, priests it was the elders bit I found difficult to comprehend. I found it impossible to apply this rule to my big sister Marie Therese who was three years older than me and therefore technically, came under the "elders" category. She was always teasing me and slyly hitting me when my mammy's back was turned, and telling my mammy about any misdemeanour I had innocently committed so I would get a telling off or a slap, while she stuck her tongue out at me and laughed, so I decided that she was exempt from this "elders" rule.

We had to learn the 10 commandments and were expected even at 6 or 7 years old to understand and obey them......

1...*Thou shalt not obey false gods...*

O.K. this one I understood...we were taught that our god was the only, one true god and any other gods were imposters there was only one real god...and he was ours.

2...*Thou shalt not put other false gods before me....*

The same as number 1

3...*Thou shalt not take the lord's name in vain....*But I heard my mammy and daddy saying. *Oh my god ya wee tinker what have ye done now.....for god's sake ...will you two shut up when I'm reading the* paper ...*oh Jesus Christ Owen would ye speak to that boy...*

So I figured that one was just for us children.

4...*Keep the Sabbath day sacred...*

This was fine by me...we would go to mass in the morning then come home, have breakfast, go for long walks "doon the shore" with my dad and go to my grannies for dinner with all my uncles, aunts and cousins then read books and listen to Jimmy Shand and his band playing Scottish country music on the radio while me and my sister danced wildly around the living room, then go to bed....no problem.

5...*Honour your father and mother...*

Of course I always honoured my father and mother...If not I got a hard slap on the bare legs.

6..*Thou shalt not murder....*My mum was always telling me that she would murder me...particularly if she caught me playing with that wee proddy across the street. She hadn't actually carried out the threat yet...but I was absolutely sure that she was capable and that one day she would.

7...*Thou shalt not commit adultery...*

"*Mammy what does commit adultery mean?*"

"*Ach away and ask yer daddy.*"

"*Daddy what does adultery mean?*"

"*Ach away and ask yer granny?*"

"*Granny whit does adultery mean?*"

"*Ach sure I don't know away and ask yer Uncle John.*"

My Uncle John had been a monk, he was a very religious man and an intellectual. Surely he would know the answer......

"*Uncle John?*"

"*Away and ask your teacher*"............

No one would answer my question. Either these adults were ignorant or there was something they were hiding from me.

I asked my big sister. She was three years older than me and was always acting so bossy and grown up and would surely come up with the answer..........

"Sure everybody knows that...you're just a silly wee boy."

"It's when a man likes another man's wife and he kisses her.".....

What???...now I was even more confused. Why on earth would a man want to kiss any woman let alone one who had been kissing another man...?

8...Thou shalt not steal....

"Well then my sister was going straight to hell because she stole one of my candy balls my mammy had bought me from Minnie Steele's sweetie shop as a special reward because I went to help her with the shopping in the High Street. I was sitting at the table counting them and my big sister walked past and just took one without my permission.

9...Thou shalt not bear false witness against thy neighbour...

I think this meant you shouldn't tell lies about a neighbour...well what about when Jim Walsh who sat beside me in class, told the teacher I had copied his arithmetic answers and I really hadn't and I got a telling off from Mrs Connolly.

10...Thou shalt not covet thy neighbour's wife, his house, his servants, his donkey....

"Mammy????....Daddy???.....Uncle John???.... Marie Therese?"...

We were told that us wee catholic children couldn't be held responsible for breaking any of these commandments until we had reached the age of reason.

Seven years old was the designated age when we were considered to have enough worldly knowledge and experience to know the difference between right and wrong and that we were incapable of committing any sins until we reached that age. We were told that if a child died before seven years old they automatically went straight to heaven to be an angel and live for eternity as one of god's personal helpers. I remember being very disappointed on 24th December 1958 when, on my seventh birthday I realized that it was now too late and I could never break any of the commandments and must obey all the complicated rules of the Catholic Church and be judged on judgement day along with all the other sinners. My passport to eternal happiness in heaven at god's side as one of his wee angels had expired and from this day on breaking any of these commandments was a mortal sin and I would have a big black mark on my soul and if I died with one of these stains on my soul I would have to go straight to "purgatory" which, we were taught was a kind of waiting room where you had to stay for an undisclosed period of time until you had repented your sins and your wee soul was then spotless and considered by god to be clean enough to be allowed to enter into his kingdom of heaven.

During my primary school years I was a model student and loved school. Obeyed the teachers, learned the three "Rs" and achieved high marks in most subjects although reading, writing and art were my favourites and I passed all my exams with flying colours.

My years at wee West Bridgend Primary School passed happily and it wasn't long before I was sitting my eleven plus exam in preparation for the "big school"

The eleven plus exam was designed to determine your academic skills and the pass grade decided which class you would continue in secondary school. My pass was a "B" so I would enter into St Patricks High School in 1B.

I was excited about this forthcoming adventure and so it was I finally left my happy, carefree days at "wee school" in July 1962,prepared for the school holidays and waited impatiently to start the" big school" in September and looking forward to wearing long trousers for the first time in my life.

Now the stories about the "big school" which were recounted to us wee boys by the big boys were terrifying. We were warned that the teachers were vicious, slap-happy sadists who would shout at you whack you around the back of the head and slap your hands with a big,thick,hard leather belt for the slightest reason. Surely this couldn't possibly be true?

After the kind and loving teachers at my primary school who only ever shouted at us pupils for slurping our milk. I was about to have the biggest shock of my short innocent life. We were treated to fearsome stories about the discipline in the big school and in particular about Rinty Monaghan the headmaster and chief torturer

Of course, surely this was all talk and rumours intended to frighten us.

None of these horror stories could possibly be true....or could they?

I was about to find out................

St Patrick's High School

When I say that William B Monaghan, headmaster and chief scaremonger in charge of St Patrick's High School intimidated me, it isn't a boast, it wasn't too difficult. At 11 years old, I was the tall, shy, gangly, nervous new boy in the school. Also the skinniest, weakest and by far the most frightened.

Rinty was his nickname, headmaster and frightener-in-chief, was a bear in a black gown.

As headmaster of St Patrick's High School in our small town of Dumbarton, Rinty set the strict standards and the moral compass.

For more than 20 years, he took grubby, cheeky wee Scottish boys like me and turned them into proud, well- mannered young men who were well- educated and even semi-civilised, whether we liked it or not.

He achieved this with a combination of intimidation, charm, wit, and intelligence, and a rock solid personality.

Not to mention, of course, his dreaded, thick, leather, double tongued strap. He ruled us not so much with a rod of iron as with a strap of heavy leather.

To this day, you will find an endless number of ex-students my age who swear their lives were vastly enhanced by his early influence. Me included.

When I arrived in St Patrick's High School, 11 years old, fresh faced and naive, he was already a legend.

It was my first day at the "the big school," the day I had been looking forward to for a long time, my first day wearing long trousers, I was feeling so grown-up. After we had said the obligatory morning prayers in assembly, I offered to help the teachers to collect the ancient, tubular steel chairs and stack them against the wall. In my excitement and enthusiasm I scraped one on the wall. Then followed my first experience of Rinty and his legendary, murderous leather strap.

Now this wasn't some freshly painted, pristine wall. Oh no...this wall was as old as the school itself and was in dire need of some care and attention not to mention a lick of paint, as was the whole school. Unfortunately for me this catastrophic error was spotted by one of the teachers I was helping. How this eagle eyed teacher had noticed that my chair had put a new scratch on this wall already full of centuries old scratches and dents I will never know, but notice he did and he wasn't happy......

"You son, the long lanky boy"

"Who me? Sir?"

"Yes, you skinny malinky long legs, what's your name son?"

"Err, Err Mcloughlin sir....Joseph Mcloughlin."

Well Mcloughlin, get yourself down that corridor and wait outside the headmaster's office, and when you go in tell him you are there because you caused wilful damage to school property.

"wilful damage"?...I was confused....naive and fresh from primary school I had never heard this adjective "wilful" before, we never learned this word in our English class with Miss Connolly, but I was pretty damn certain by the tone of the teacher's voice, that it wasn't good.

I was always taught never to show disrespect, talk back or be cheeky to any adults particularly teachers and always do as I was told without hesitation or question.

So off I went to the headmaster's office obediently and fearfully, to await my fate.

I was about to meet the mythical Rinty the headmaster who had a reputation as a cruel, strict, sadist which I had heard about long before I had arrived there on my first day. I was about to discover that all the horror stories from the older boys were not the stuff of fiction after all ,and at that moment whilst waiting in the queue for the torturer in chief ,all these horror stories were swilling around inside my head and I was secretly hoping and praying that they really were all wildly exaggerated.

Surely he didn't beat boys black and blue until they screamed for their mother?

Surely he didn't break students' fingers with the force of the strokes if they pulled their hands away?

Surely he didn't throw his head back laughing wildly like a madman, while he delivered the deadly strokes of his belt......

Surely he didn't sleep with his beloved strap, and as some said, wrap it around his erect penis..........

Surely he didn't eat babies for breakfast?......

Surely not..., surely not... surely not........................

Whilst I was waiting outside Rinty's study to receive my punishment for this "wilful damage" another two new boys arrived.

So now there were three of us nervous convicts on death row, trying to appear brave we were swapping stories as to why we were there.

One boy had committed the mortal sin of not addressing a teacher as "Sir". Whilst the other had been one minute late for assembly and had been spotted sneaking in by another eagle eyed teacher. So now here we were outside awaiting our trial without jury and inevitable guilty sentence and punishment, we could hear some muffled voices coming from inside the study behind the thick, dark oak door and straining our ears we tried to pick out some conversation. Our concentration was suddenly shattered by the horrendous, sickening sound of leather on skin which was repeated six times with each sound being followed by a loud shriek of pain coming from the poor victim who was on the receiving end of this singular punishment. Now we were physically shaking, when the door finally opened and out came the new boy victim. He was crying and sobbing uncontrollably whilst holding his hands under his armpits and pleading for his mummy so we couldn't see if he still had all his fingers or not.....

We three criminals exchanged glances at each other and I'm sure we observed the same look of fear and dread in each other's eyes. I was next and as I entered the chamber of horrors I was immediately struck by the darkness of the interior.

It was a small office with only one bare light bulb illuminating the dark oak lined walls and with a wooden floor which squeaked and creaked as I stepped into the chamber of horrors. It smelled of old leather and furniture polish which was the same smell as my grannie's living room on a Saturday morning when she polished the table...oh how I wished I was in that living room now with my grannie safe and warm. How could two places evoking such opposite sentiments have the same smell?

Hanging on the wall behind a huge oak desk there was a large portrait of Rinty, smiling in full, black gown and purple sash with his graduation hat at a jaunty angle and the tassel hanging down over the side of his smug, smiling face and holding some kind of diploma. Behind the desk was an enormous, well worn, leather armchair, where, I was sure, Rinty would sit plotting his torturous punishments for any insignificant little boys who had the audacity to disobey the rules of his school. To the right stood an enormous bookcase full of old, well read books. Now, I loved reading books and at that moment I really wanted to have a good look at them, take them out one by one, blow off the dust and spend some time flicking through the time worn pages.

But now my thoughts were abruptly interrupted............

"Why are you here boy?"... Rinty said with an air of authoritative indifference.

His loud voice boomed and resounded off the dark oak walls of the small dim office....

"Err, Err, a teacher sent me here to see you...ssssir?"...I replied in a trembling voice.

"Oh did he now.....and what crime have you committed so horrendous and despicable that a teacher would send you here to waste my valuable time and interrupt my busy day"

"Err he said that I had "wilfully" damaged school property...sir?"

I continued in a squeaky voice......

"I was helping him to put away some chairs after assembly and he said I scratched a wall with one of the chairs.

"WILFULLY" ...you say? "WILFULLY"??..... Now with him emphasising this new word, it sounded a hundred times more serious.....

"Damage to school property is a very serious offence and as such must have serious punishment so that stupid little new boys like you learn the valuable lesson that every action has a consequence and don't ever repeat their mistakes."

I wanted to tell him that I promise never ever to touch the school property again never mind damage it "wilfully" or otherwise but now I was speechlessly transfixed by the huge solid brown, thick, leather belt which was resting on top of the desk and for which he now slowly reached. Picking it up and resting it on his shoulder, ready for action. Was it a figment of my fertile imagination of was he actually caressing and stroking it lovingly? In any case I was now more scared than ever and my eyes were now glued to this object of fear......

"Put out your hands boy".... He pointed the belt at my trembling hands.

I decided to take an optimistic view of the situation so I put my hands out separately about 6 inches apart.... a big mistake.......

"'Ah...so we have a joker in our midst eh? What is your name boy?'...he growled. .

'Err, Err....JJJoseph, sir,' I squeaked.

"Joseph? Joseph What???"...I presume you have a surname boy". His baritone voice boomed and resounded off the oak panel walls.

"Err Err Err Mcloughlin ssssir."

Well Mcloughlin...forget about your first name...in this school troublesome, destructive little vandals like you don't have first names...your name from now on will be Mcloughlin."

'So Mcloughlin, be kind enough to put out your hands together one on top of the other and with your palms up."

His politeness, calmness and matter of fact attitude was in direct contrast to the turmoil going on inside my head. He raised the strap above his head and brought it down with all his strength and with perfect aim onto my trembling palms. The next thing I heard and felt was the sickening thud of leather as it made contact with my tender young skin. The searing pain surging up my outstretched hands and up my arms....Six times.

"Only six for now because this is your first day, '" he said in a matter-of-fact way....... "Oh lucky me!"... I thought as I bit my trembling bottom lip to stop myself from crying.

I opened the door and walked out of the study avoiding any eye contact with the two, white faced, open mouthed fellow victims waiting their turns outside in the corridor.

This was my first day at St Patrick's High secondary school the day that I had been looking forward to for months. My first day at the "big" school, my first day wearing long trousers........It was only five minutes to nine...... I still hadn't even reached my first classroom.

After my first five years at West Bridgend Primary school, being taught by kind-hearted teachers, where the teachers only ever shouted at us and would never have dreamt of hitting any child in their charge......this truly was a baptism by fire.

Rinty ran a tight ship. No running, no shouting, no fighting, no cheek, no disrespect to teachers, no speaking unless you're spoken to. We had to wear our uniforms at all times and call every teacher Sir or Miss. To be caught with your school blazer unbuttoned in the school or even in the street outside the school was practically a hanging offence and often a concerned stranger seeing you in the street with your blazer undone would whisper some friendly advice in your ear...

"Dae up yer jaikit son before any of the teachers see you"

Rinty called everyone, teachers as well as boys, by their surnames. Everyone called him Headmaster.

If a teacher ordered you to go and stand outside the classroom doors for any reason, you had better hope and pray that Rinty wouldn't happen to be patrolling along the corridors. The terrifying possibility of him finding you outside of a classroom during lessons would lead to an interrogation as to why you weren't in class, and would certainly be a good enough reason to order you to go and wait outside his study for him to return. I don't know what was worse, the waiting or the strappings. Standing there waiting for him to come back was the scariest feeling in the world.

I would sit quietly and strain my ears to listen for his approaching footsteps. To this day, the squeak of leather shoes on polished wooden floors breaks me out in a cold sweat.

He held us in a fearful fascination and in a continuous state of alert.

One day, our teacher had to leave the class for a few minutes and in those few unsupervised minutes we took full advantage of the situation, everyone became over-excited. Loud voices screeched, insults were shouted, fists were flying when suddenly the door flew open. The doorway darkened. …and there HE was… "Follow me, all of you", he shouted, his voice shaking the walls.

Degraded, trembling with fear, and squeaking like mice, we all obediently followed him to his study where he strapped all 30 of us,…… in alphabetical order.

By the time he got to the last boy called Graham Woods, he had adopted his usual scary-funny attitude.

"I expect you think I'm getting tired, Woods, my son. Well let's see about that, shall we" And he strapped poor Graham harder just to show that he wasn't.

One day, Woods said he was fed up with always being last and was going to change his name by deed poll to Anderson just so he didn't have to always be last in line.

Today, all this corporal punishment of young children sounds cruel and barbaric and of course it was. But you have to remember that at that time at home we were all accustomed to smacks over the head, the legs, the backside or any other convenient part of our anatomy within reach of our parents, adults, teachers, priests or neighbours. So we were used to being the targets of violence.

In a strange sort of way, we were proud to have such a fearsome figure as Rinty as our headmaster.

If the continual strappings were a challenge, then his tongue-lashings were even worse. They could cause bigger blisters than his strap.

One day four of us were summoned before him for…. I think….suspected not paying attention in Latin class, he observed in a friendly fashion that we were all straight A, intelligent boys and he expressed his sadness and disappointment at the fact that we were now standing before him accused of this serious misdemeanour.

Then, with the twisted, maniacal smile that signalled that a tongue lashing was on its way, he added: "As the intellectual cream of our school, you will know that the cream is not the only thing which floats to the top."

He paused for dramatic effect…… "So does the shit."

Then he proceeded to strap each one of us six times and made us conjugate aloud the verb "to be" in Latin.

However, despite the constant threat of corporal punishment, as boys we had a natural gift for devilment and bad behaviour that was hard to contain. Somehow, despite all the regulations, now and again we attempted to break loose.

Whenever we saw a weakness in any teacher, we struck.

Our new music teacher, Mr Smith, for example, had shown signs that he wanted to be our friend and for us to like him. He might as well have given us a loaded gun.

When he next tried to test our voices by singing the scales, as he sat at the piano, one by one we sang in silly voices…….

"Do, Re, Mi, Fa, So, La, Ti, Do"…..Too high, too low, baritone grunts, trilling sopranos. We thought it was fantastic, hilarious fun.

Poor old Smithy cracked. He began throwing books around the room and copies of sheet music at us, shouting….

"You rotten little toe rags, I hate you all!'"…It was wonderful. We had won a victory.

We never saw him again. Triumphantly, we waited for his replacement, hand-picked as always, by Rinty the headmaster.

Jackie Pickup was our new music teacher who eventually arrived and tried to test our voices. We repeated all our silly noises just as we had with old Smithy before.

Quietly and without a word or look of anger he stood up and began handing out sheets of blank music paper, lightly marked with hundreds of tiny, narrow lines.

'What do we have to do with these, sir?' we asked him.

Write out 100 times "I must obey and respect the teacher", and don't cross any of the lines. And hand them back to me first thing in the morning and any boy who hasn't completed this simple task will be sent to the headmaster.

"But sir… that's going to take us hours,"

"Yes precisely….. Now, let me hear those sweet voices."

We knew when we were beaten. Mr Pickup was our music teacher and choirmaster for many years.

Despite the strappings, or perhaps because of them we became respectful, obedient and well educated students.

William B Monaghan was an exceptional headmaster. He provided us with a controlled and disciplined environment in which the expectation was that we would toil, learn and thrive.

We did just that. Moreover, we actually learned to enjoy it.

Even the strappings were insignificant. The pain disappeared after a couple of hours, the overriding messages, study, learn, behave yourself and respect authority — lasted a lifetime.

I understood that Rinty used his strap and his savage tongue simply to control us boys permanently on the brink of mutiny. In the end, I found myself boasting about his severity.

By the time I left St Patrick's High School I realised that I had experienced a golden age. I was lucky to have experienced the prime of William B Monaghan.

The difference between the sixties and today was that then the grown-ups were in charge of the growing ups.

There were other differences. When I was a teenager, I didn't know….had never heard of…. anyone who had been robbed, burgled, raped or mugged.

The local paper, the Lennox Herald, never featured any photographs of battered pensioners, blackened eyes and swollen faces, who'd been beaten up by mindless thugs in search of fun.

There were never any stories of youngsters destroying their parents' houses with Facebook parties, or girls lying in city centre gutters with their skirts over their heads in a pool of vomit.

My childhood and youth in the 50s and 60s was the last time in the U.K. when young people were expected to behave themselves, to do exactly what they were told when they were told, to comb their hair, tidy their rooms, do their homework, never be late for school and never, ever be cheeky or talk back to adults, teachers, priests or anyone in fact older than them. You listened to and respected your elders.

Unlike now when we are faced with a whole generation of couch potatoes, permanently attached by cables, playing endless, violent games on the latest electronic device ,who would rather immerse themselves in reality T.V. for hours on end, than go outside and use their imagination or do some sport or read a decent book. A generation almost entirely devoid of inventiveness, dedicated to empty materialism, a generation that conforms slavishly to universal fashions in clothes, music and technological gadgets. Nowadays we have the "I" generation who must have the latest i-phones, i-pads, i-pods, a lost generation that has nothing it can hold its head up and describe proudly as being uniquely its own idea.

Whether there was any connection between Rinty's regime, his leather strap and young people's respectful behaviour, I wouldn't know. What Rinty did to wee Dunbartonshire boys....including me....50 years ago was whatever was needed to turn us into polite, well educated, confident young men who were fully prepared to make their way in the outside world.

As for productive, no-nonsense education? .....Rinty invented it.

French Lessons

Foreign languages were never the most popular subject in our school, after all most juvenile boys in Dumbarton had problems understanding and speaking English never mind any other language...However, I always had a fascination for languages ever since I was young when we were forced to sit for two hours every Sunday and listen to a boring, monotonous mass, which I was forced to attend, delivered by a robotic priest and in Latin. I was intrigued to find out more and to understand this strange foreign language with so many unpronounceable words. So in the forlorn hope that it could make the mass more interesting I set about investigating the Latin language. My sister, who being three years older than me was already taking Latin in her school at Notre Dame High School where she was taught by catholic nuns and so I would borrow her books and pester her until she explained some of the meanings to me.

So when I went into third year at 13 years old and the option of taking languages presented itself I jumped at the chance.

Latin was taught by Chalky Neeson, an old traditional school teacher who drummed Latin verbs into our heads. We *amoed, amated and amad* enthusiastically but I figured as this was a pretty useless language in terms of future use then I gave up after a year and took up French instead.

The French teacher Miss Diamond was a frumpy, old teacher who I considered to be about 80 years old when in actual fact she was probably in her 40s.She was another old style teacher and always wore her woollen suit and thick tights and sensible shoes winter and summer, she always wore her black gown and had the ability to instil fear into any young boy who dared to speak while she was speaking, Not for her the obligatory weapon of discipline, the strap, her particular chosen favourite method of inflicting pain was the blackboard duster. These dusters were just a block of wood with a bit of sponge glued on so that the teacher could clean the chalk off the blackboard. Now this may seem a fairly innocuous weapon of punishment but Miss Diamond was gifted with perfect eyesight and an aim that would shame an SAS sniper. She could throw that duster from the front of the class next to her desk to any of the four corners of the room with outstanding accuracy, her chosen target being any boy who she suspected of not listening, talking while she was talking or any other serious misdemeanour. If that duster came flying through the air in your direction you had better pray that it's your lucky day and that the soft sponge bit hits your head first, and all you have is acute embarrassment and chalk dust on your head because if not then you would certainly go home with a giant bruise and have a king-size headache for the rest of the day. Miss Diamond´s legendary duster throwing was of Olympic standard and would always be accompanied by the request for the victim to please return the duster to her and as a further penance…. clean the board.

Now as I said Miss Diamond was old so it was inevitable that one day she would retire or move to a more peaceful school where she could relax and see out the rest of her teaching career in peace and quiet with students who paid attention to everything she said and who actually gave a damn.

So it was that we were told one day at assembly by headmaster Rinty Monaghan that Miss Diamond would be leaving and that she would be replaced with a native French teacher Miss Deauville.

Now I for one was happy because Miss Diamond's method of teaching French was with the aid of course books filled with grammar, verbs and vocabulary which we had to learn parrot fashion, we then had tests to make sure that we understood all this vocabulary but never had the opportunity to practice and I for one was keen to practice speaking too.

In our French class were about 12 boys who mostly had chosen French because they wanted to learn a foreign language there were also one or two misfits who had chosen it in order to escape some more difficult subject such as algebra, or physics.

There were rumours going around the school that the new French teacher was young. I was sceptical about this as the youngest teacher in our school was surely 60 years old I had never seen any young teachers in our school during the previous two years and when one old codger retired or had a nervous breakdown they were immediately replaced by a similar model of the same age and sadistic character.

So the day Miss Deauville arrived was therefore a momentous day in the history of St Patrick's High School.

The system for transferring classes in our school was that the teachers had their own designated classrooms and we students changed classes depending on our next subject. This chaotic system meant that when the bell rang for the end of a lesson then 1000 crazy boys left their respective classes and moved on to their next subject class., passing through the narrow corridors in all directions. It was like the end of a football match when all the spectators were leaving and heading off in all directions to their respective homes. This system also gave boys the opportunity of social interaction or in other words to throw insults and punches or kicks at their schoolmates or enemies whilst passing them in the corridors where fights would often break out. Of course there were some supervising teachers patrolling at the same time but they couldn't possibly see everything that was going on behind their backs so there were often cries of......

"Sir, McGregor punched me Sir"

"Just keep moving boy you probably deserved it"

So this day I headed to the French class with anticipation, curious to discover what type of ugly old witch Rinty Monaghan had personally chosen to continue the torturous regime of the dearly departed Miss Diamond.

I opened the door and walked casually into the class and that is when my jaw dropped and hit the floor, for there sitting at the desk was an image of absolute beauty the likes of which I had only ever seen in the films or on the inside pages of my dad's Men Only magazine.... but without the staples.

She was beautiful, long auburn, wavy hair falling over her shoulders, she was fully made-up including fashionable eye shadow, lipstick, blusher, and the works. She was slim and best of all she really was young. She was wearing a tight thin jumper which accentuated her perfectly shaped breasts with or without the help of one of the new fashionable padded bras which all the girls were wearing at this time. But it was when she stood up that my blood pressure really hit boiling point...she was wearing a pink mini skirt, now this was the mid-sixties and miniskirts were the height of fashion, but I had never seen a teacher wearing one, did she not realize that she was teaching a class of young pubescent, horny little bastards with turbulent hormones running wild through every part of our testosterone fuelled bodies? Obviously she was under the illusion that we were children...a big mistake.

I couldn't take my eyes off her. I'm sure that if I could have dragged my gaze away for a second to look around at the rest of the class I would have found that they were all as transfixed as me. I'm certain at this point that a little bit of saliva was running down my chin.

I estimated her age to be about 25-30 other boys speculated later that she was only 19-20 and was a student teacher and only a temporary replacement who would disappear when the real ugly old ratbag would surely arrive as her replacement to make our lives a misery.

The vision of beauty spoke......

"Pleeessss seet down boysss...now pleeesss"...

Please?.... What??...were my ears deceiving me??'

Did she really say **please**?

Please was never a word I had heard any teacher in our school use before.

"Goooot morning boysss.., my name eeesss Claudia Deauville and I am your new French teacher"

Claudia...Claudia......Claudia.......what a name....what an accent ...what a beauty... I was head over heels in love

This was a complete revelation...no teacher had ever introduced themselves to us before and definitely never by their first name.

I was pinching myself to see if this was real and not just another one of my wet dreams.

The news of the arrival of this goddess in a mini skirt circulated faster than my hand went down my trousers and soon there were more than 30 boys in my French class, with all the front desks with the grandstand views being taken up by the school's tough bullies. However this didn't prove much of a problem because Miss Deauville or "Mademoiselle Claudia" as she demanded we call her, insisted on sharing her beauty with everyone by walking up and down the rows of desks whilst conjugating French verbs and whilst tapping out the rhythm with a ruler. so we all got a close up view of her gorgeous long legs and she would often pause at the front of the class to bend over to pick up a piece of chalk, when she did this there was always the deafening sound of moaning as the class as one took a sharp intake of breath quickly followed by the shuffling of bums on seats as hands rearranging the space inside trousers.....

Every week she brought into class a French magazine called CaVa and she would positions herself sitting facing the class and read an extract which we were supposed to write what she was reading. Nobody was listening, nobody was writing. Sitting there with her legs crossed, wearing a mini skirt which was slowly moving up her thighs, the last thing on our pubescent minds was to listen to what she was saying, her dictation fell on deaf ears. All eyeballs were extended and focused on that upwardly mobile mini skirt until the tantalising moment when it arrived at the stocking top, when a collective moan echoed around the classroom.

"Now repeat after me booyyssss"....the verb *"to be"*

Je suis...tu es...il est....elle est....nous sommes....vous etes...ils sont...elles sont...

No matter how hard we tried to impress her with our linguistic skills

Our Scottish accents were just not up to this French pronunciation

Jeyswees...tooess...eeelest...elest...nooossomms...voooosetis...eeelsont...elsont.

We were a disaster but Mademoiselle Claudia was very patient.

"Now I want to know all your names... she said in her soft, sexy French accent.

"I weeeelll ask you een French... ¿comment vous appelez vous? I want you to answer "J'm apelle...followed by your name"

"You, tall, skinny boy"....she was pointing her ruler and talking to me...and she just called me tall, skinny boy...this was a huge improvement on the names invented by all the other teachers...this was the first time I had been called anything other than..."lang streak o misery". Skinny malinky longlegs"....skin and bone left alone"...

"Comment vous appelez vous"...she whispered in her sexy French accent.

"Je mapelle..."Mcloughlin ...m m mademoiselle Claudia..."...I stuttered.

"Mon dui! Sacre bleu! Garcon!"... She shouted,"

"Your name een thees class ees "Joseph"...now repeat after me...

"Je m'appelle Joseph".

"Er.er... bbbut mademoiselle, were not allowed to use our first names with teachers"

She walked slowly towards me, my heart was pounding in my chest, my hands were sweating, I went red in the face as she approached, she put her beautiful face close to mine...so close I could smell her French perfume,...her pointy breasts were almost touching my chest.....I was blushing, and sweating...something damp and warm leaked out of my willy and dripped down my leg......she looked me straight in the eye........

"In MY class I will do as I weeshh and in MY class all boys will be called by their FIRST names. And you will be Monsieur Joseph.....do you understand"

....*"oui, oui mademoiselle Claudia...tres bien...oui, oui.oui!!!"*

Oh my god...this was unbelievable......when Rinty gets to hear about this...she will be gone for sure, sent to another school far away, with lucky adolescent boys who can be called by their first names..

But she wasn't ...she stayed and taught me French for two years and unknown to her gave me many moments of lonely, private sexual fantasies.

She was a real, live goddess and we were putty in her hands, she didn't need any form of physical discipline, no strap, no flying dusters, no slaps on the back of the head, we were like little angels in her class. Anyone who misbehaved would receive a beating from the class bullies who dished out the punishment in the playground later on her behalf. She had us singing Frere Jacques and Sur le Pont d'Avignon in three part harmony, reading Mon Oncle Cassimere out loud and our conversations were peppered with "si'l vous plait and merci beaucoup ...surely this should have been an example to Rinty of how to teach and control a bunch of adolescent scallywags, the answer was obvious....... get rid of all the sadistic, old ugly teachers and replace them with young beautiful ones who could mesmerise us with their beautiful legs and breasts, and teach us and keep us under control at the same time.

Without doubt Mademoiselle Claudia was the most popular teacher in our school. Particularly when she arrived in the playground car park each day in her little green, French Citroen 2cv car. We calculated that if we stood in a certain position in the car park we would surely be treated to a bird's eye view of her opening the door and swinging her long, slender legs out of her car, so we hatched a plan with military precision .The morning arrived, we were nervously waiting in our pre- planned position, hands down trousers, her little green 2cv car arrived, she reversed into her parking spot, our level of excitement was now hitting boiling point, the moment was finally here we waited in anticipation, she stopped her car, opened the door and got out...........

What the Fuck???…We saw nothing…In our juvenile stupidity as wee naïve Dumbarton boys we hadn't taken into account that her car was French and as such, naturally, had the steering wheel on the opposite side so while we were all waiting with baited breath, she elegantly stepped out of the driver's door on the other side. Disappointed but not put off we re-planned, re-grouped and changed our tactics and waited on the correct side in future. The doors on this car opened backwards and so when she opened the door she had to swing her long slim legs out much to the excitement of the waiting crowd of sweaty, horny young lechers. I am convinced that she knew about this adolescent adulation and the power she held over us as she would always exaggerate the leg show performance and flash a big smile and a *"bonjour garcones"* at us.

Her classroom was on the first floor and there were two flights of stairs she had to climb to get there and so it was that every morning after assembly crowds would gather outside the staff room, which was on the ground floor and groups of excited young pubescent schoolboys derived many hours of pleasure by hanging around and waiting for her to come out and walk up the stairs in her mini skirt to go to her class. The trick was to wait for about 5 seconds until she was at the top of the first flight of stairs then innocently follow her up at a safe distance meanwhile getting adoring eyes filled with the titillating glimpse of her stocking tops and knickers, later to be boasted about in the playground and replayed over and over again like a slow motion movie when alone in the toilets.

Physical Education

Our P.E. teacher was another St Pat's legend...us new boys had heard all the horror stories about Jack Gilroy...known as "Jaffa"

Jaffa was a psychopath and taught P.E.

He was a mad keen sportsman and expected all his pupils to have the same level of love for sport as him. He had played professional football in his younger years and it was well known that his ambition was to have the best school football team in Scotland. He was a powerhouse, very fit and like all other teachers he didn't tolerate any break of his strict rules and came down like a ton of bricks on any boy who broke them.

Turning up for his P.E. class a few seconds late or without the correct clothing was a serious major crime and the perpetrator would be subject to one of his barbarous forms of punishment.

His territory was the gymnasium and the sports field.

In St Pats we only had one sport...football, if you were a good footballer you were favoured by Jaffa, if not he tried his best to turn you into one, if you had no skills in football he gave up and ignored you

I fell into the latter category.

Being tall and skinny I was never physically designed to play football. Jaffa tried me out a couple of times at all positions before finally abandoning hope.......

"Right Mcloughlin with them long legs and long arms I think we'll try you in goal today."

So there I stood in my shorts and vest, skinny gangly legs and skinny arms it was virtually impossible to tell any difference between me and the goalposts. I looked like a pair of braces.....

"Right Lanky Legs.... stand in the centre of the goal and the other boys will take shots at you from the penalty spot all you have to do is stop the ball from going into the net."..

I looked with trepidation at this penalty spot he was indicating and it looked very close...too close........

This is going to hurt I thought...I was terrified.

Balls flew at me from all directions. I cowered and hid my face in my hands, my arms completely disconnected from my brain were flailing around like windmills. I dived a couple of times, well when I say dived I mean I gently leaned over in the general direction of the moving ball and stuck out my arms in a feeble attempt to stop it going into the net. When a low ball came straight at me I was so slow that by the time I reached down I was always two seconds too late. The other problem with my goalkeeping skills was that my legs being so long and standing in the centre of the goal with my legs apart it was easy for anyone to kick a ball straight through my open legs.

My spectacular performances were always greeted with screams of laughter and shouts of.....

"Shut yer legs here comes a bus"

"Yer supposed to catch the ball BEFORE it goes into the net. ...ya eedjit."

"Hey skinny malinky long legs....keep yer eye on the ball....not up the chimney"

"Hey big yin....away an get yer eyes tested."

When I picked the ball out of the back of the net for the umpteenth time and tried to kick it back out to the other players my legs were so long that the message from my brain didn't reach them until a few seconds later. I always missed it and ended up kicking fresh air whilst the ball bounced back into the back of the net.

Jaffa tried me out of goal playing in defence. He was under the misplaced illusion that I could stop the attackers from getting to the goal...

When the attackers started running full speed with the ball in my direction and terrified of being hit in the face by the flying ball I turned my back, buried my face in my hands and crouched low. The attackers, smelling my fear simply pretended to kick the ball and when I turned away and covered my face for protection they walked past me and headed for the goal.

I was a total disaster.

He tried me as a forward........

"Right big yin...were going to use your height as an advantage."

"Stand here in front of the goal and when a high cross come over, you jump up and header the ball into the net."

Header??...He said header???...using my head to hit a hard, fast moving ball was not my idea of fun and would surely cause me a considerable amount of pain...was my first thought.

My second was...what if I miss it with the top of my head and it hits my face instead? This was going to hurt a lot.

So when the high balls came flying over I was so scared that I let it fly past my head straight to the feet or the hands of the goalkeeper.

Jaffa finally, in exasperation gave up on me, as a lost cause. It was obvious that I was never going to be good enough be in the football team. I was secretly quite pleased about this as it meant I could save myself from further acute embarrassment and stay in the warm gym instead of freezing my balls off outside on the football pitch.

Jaffa was, however, intent on making me fit and designed a circuit of the gym which me and the other hopeless non-footballers could do whilst he was outside on the pitch training the elite.

Jaffa never used the leather strap on us...oh no...The strap was for sissies. His preferred weapons of torture were any heavy object which he found near his hand at the time of the offence.

He would throw football boots one after the other at your head or a big heavy ball he called a "medicine ball" full force at your stomach, your face, your back, your testicles, anywhere, in fact he decided would cause the most pain.

I was on the receiving end of this punishment many times as he endeavoured to turn this *"long skinny useless lanky waste of space"* as he called me, into a muscle bound Adonis.

He would sometimes appear suddenly in the gym to check that we outcasts were doing the circuit training which he had ordered......

"Mcloughlin why are you sitting on the floor instead of hanging from the bars doing leg curls like I told you?"

"Well sir I am tired and I needed to stop to catch my breath."

"Right get on them bars and hang by your feet upside down facing me ...NOW!!"

When after a few minutes I managed to get myself into the upside down hanging position as he had ordered and with my arms hanging down almost touching the floor he launched the big heavy ball from a distance of about two yards straight at my stomach.

Doubling up with pain I fell off the bars and lying in agony on the floor at his feet, he dropped the ball again this time, just for fun, on my head.

"Now next time I tell you to do a non-stop circuit...that means non stop

Understand son?"

"Oooohhhhh.....yyyyyyeesss sir"....

"Now get up and give me 10 sit ups"

I was lucky, as a tall boy he couldn't perform one of his favourite tortures on me

This particular method of discipline was reserved for smaller boys, he would pick one up by the ears until their feet were about 2 feet off the ground and their face was level with his, explain in a matter of fact way that the heinous crime they had committed would not be tolerated and that they should in future obey his every command to the letter, then he would elevate them until his arms were above his head still holding them by the ears, then let go.

As his unfortunate victim dropped towards the floor he would then bring both palms together effectively slapping them on both ears at the same time as they fell to the floor.

This was particularly effective on a cold winter day when the ears were frozen and also had the added advantage of leaving the victim's ears ringing and red raw for the rest of the day.

Under Jaffa Gilroy St Patrick's High was one of the top school football teams in the country, recognised as worthy opponents and feared by many and won many trophies.

We were all very proud of our team and would all stand in the freezing cold on a Saturday morning cheering from the side-lines and travel on Saturday afternoons on the school bus to all the away games. Cheering wildly at the end when our team was awarded another cup.

The whole school would stand and applaud our conquering heroes in assemblies when Rinty would announce another win for the school team and Jaffa and his superstar protégées were then paraded on the stage with Jaffa making a speech about how proud he was of his boys and his football team.

I was jealous and wished that I had the ability to kick a football into a goal or enough coordination required to even save one from going straight passed me into the back of the net.

My opportunity to be applauded on stage would come soon...but not for football.

Music

Jackie Pickup was our music teacher. He was a tall, lovely gentle man with a very loud voice...a breath of fresh air compared to all the other sadistic teachers.

Music was one of my favourite subjects. I loved learning how to read and write music, I learned how to play guitar and recorder and piano and Jackie Pickup encouraged me to practice and improve. He encouraged some of us to form a band. Me, John Madden, John White and Joe Docherty sang and played guitars together. We sang all the Beatles hits like "Money" "This Boy", and of course "She Loves You" and also The Bachelors, "Ramona" which we sang in three part harmony. We continued our practice sessions most days in my house after school. My dad had discovered and old piano which someone was throwing away and he brought it home. Me and my sister had a lot of fun trying learning to play it but my friend Pat Dobbin was a fantastic pianist and could play any song by ear, so he was recruited into our supergroup which we called "The Prophets". Our drum kit was made from bin lids covered with wallpaper, plain side out, and on front we wrote "The Prophets" The side drums were biscuit tins and the symbol a pot lid. The "symbol" was suspended from our budgie cage stand so wee Joey had to be evicted during practise sessions and allowed to fly around the house whilst we used his home as a makeshift symbol stand. We thought we were fantastic and would be as famous as The Beatles one day, however, we could only play our concerts in my house because that was where the piano and drum kit were so we would invite all our friends and families to come over and of course they politely applauded and cheered each song. We gave up after a while because the drum kit was continually braking and the piano went out of tune, and so ended our short-lived music careers.

Jackie Pickup taught us how to sing and I never once saw him use any form of physical punishment on any student. His favoured method of discipline was to make us write lines. For example, if we didn't pay attention to him he made us write a hundred times "I must pay attention in class" at home and bring it to him the next day. He knew that strapping us boys had very little effect as we were so used to it and it was over in 2 minutes, made us resentful and we had no respect for the teacher. Writing these lines took hours at home and also had the side effect of alerting your parents that you had misbehaved in class.

"What's that yer writing son?"

"Oh nothing mammy just some homework"

"Just homework........ Are you telling me lies?"

"No mammy its homework honest"

"Well...you usually do yer homework in 10 minutes and you've been writing now for 3 hours".

So we behaved.

Music was an optional subject and so most of the boys in Jackie's class were there through choice and because they wanted to learn which was also the case in Art,

So in music we were all keen to learn and hardly ever misbehaved. I can only remember one time I got the hundred lines punishment. That was one day when Jackie had to leave the class for a few minutes and he put me in charge.

"Now Joseph I have to go out for a few minutes so I'm putting you in charge of the class. Make sure that the class is quiet and continue with transcribing the music I have written on the board."

"Yes sir, of course sir"

So he left the class.

The natural instinct of every pupil in our school in any class was when there was an absence of a teacher this was the opportunity to release all our pent up energy.

Immediately some boys took advantage of the situation and started running around and climbing on desks.

"Stop it lads"...... I said with all the authority I could muster.

Of course they ignored me and so I tried another method

"Please lads" I pleaded..."*you know if Mr Pickup comes back we will all get lines."*

No response.

I tried shouting...the more I shouted the louder they shouted.

Suddenly the door opened and Jackie appeared.

"What do you think you are all doing!!?"...he screamed

"Joseph come out here"

He made me stand in front facing the class, he stood behind me with his hands on my shoulders.

"Why did you all start shouting and running around when I was away?"

Well sir....*Joseph tried to tell us to be quiet but he isn't a teacher sir......*

So we don't need to obey him"

Now he turned to me..."*Joseph I put you in a position of trust and you let me down"*

I was devastated and totally ashamed that I had disappointed my favourite teacher

"Joseph ....you will write out a hundred times "I take responsibility for my failure to control the class"

"But what about the rest of the class sir........they should get lines too."

"Well I didn't put them in charge Joseph....I put you in charge so you must take full responsibility."

That is what I loved about Jackie Pickup...he was fair and I understood perfectly the lesson he was teaching me.

Later most of the class apologised to me for the incident and some even offered to share the line writing with me.

I brought the lines back to him the next day

"Joseph ...why are some of these lines in different handwriting...did someone help you?"

I couldn't tell him a lie...."*Yes sir"*

"Who helped you Joseph?"

"I can't tell you sir ....I accept full responsibility and if you give me more lines I will accept the punishment. But I am not telling you the names."

He looked me straight in the eyes….."*Well done, Joseph*"

"*You have demonstrated true leadership, your classmates shared your lines because you showed the qualities of a leader and I am proud of you.*"

I was choked…I walked back to my desk beaming with pride.

Mr Pickup was determined to improve the standing of our school in the subject of music so he decided to form a school choir.

He put up notices around the school announcing his plan and that he would be auditioning boys to discover if this idea could be a future possibility.

Every day at lunchtime he would audition potential choristers.

I was already singing in the church choir. Every Sunday we would sing the mass in Latin and Mrs McGhee the choir leader being a friend of the school had told Mr Pickup that she had a few boys in her choir who he should consider and she was confident that would be an asset to the choir as long as they could still sing at church.

So six of us were chosen by Jackie on Mrs McGhee's recommendation. The audition was a formality and all we had to do was sing the scales in tune. I had a sweet enough voice and passed the audition.

The choir was formed and we were soon practicing a couple of times a week after school.

Jackie announced one day that we would be entering the west of Scotland school choir competition. This competition was held every year with regional heats and then the final in Edinburgh between the two finalists.

We sailed through all the heats and reached the finals.

In the assembly before the final we were paraded on stage in front of the whole school and had to sing the school hymn…..

St Patricks forever

St Patricks forever

We´ll keep now our heritage and guard it evermore

St Patricks forever

St Patricks forever

We'll keep now our heritage for ever more.

The final was between us and a school called St Pius and was held in Craig Halls in Edinburgh.

It was judged by a panel of music teachers from Scottish universities.

Although all of us were nervous we were proud to be taking part in such a prestigious event and two buses full of our supporters had travelled from Dumbarton to cheer us on.

We sang our hearts out, conducted by Mr Pickup and won the competition.

I was so proud, we had won a trophy for the school.

The following Monday in assembly we were paraded on the stage with Jackie Pickup and Rinty Monaghan both making speeches of praise…… the whole school cheered and applauded.

Runty came around each boy and presented us with a diploma and shook our hands and told us and the whole school how proud he was of us and how we had brought honour to our school….what a difference from our first meeting on my first day a wee scared skinny new boy trembling with fear in his office getting six slaps with his strap for *wilfully* damaging school property now here I was 3 years later shaking that same hand and receiving words of praise for honouring the school.

As we left the assembly hall Jack Gilroy stopped me in the corridor…….

"Mcloughlin…ya lang streak of misery…..you're useless at football….but I always knew you would be good at something one day"…..he said with a big smile accompanied by a hard slap on the back of my head.

A photographer from the local paper "the Lennox Herald" took pictures of the choir posing with Rinty, Jackie Pickup and the trophy and the next week my mum was showing all the neighbours her wee son, with his school tie twisted and his "Beatle" haircut in the group photo.

The trophy and the photo were displayed in the school assembly hall for all to see…..right next to the trophies of Jaffa's football team.

English

My first year English teacher was Mr Toomey. He was an uninspiring sadist much like most of the other teachers and his teaching methods lacked interest, I hated his English class. We had to learn and conjugate parrot fashion regular and irregular verbs, learn grammar rules for conditionals, comparatives, superlatives, modal verbs etc. He gave us weekly grammar exams and if we failed to remember the past participle of any irregular verb it was hands out and six of the best. He wrote sentences on the board and we had to identify the subject, the object, the verb, the adjectives...it wasn't too difficult for me and I was completely bored stiff.

The classes were tedious and only resulted in most of us students losing interest along with the will to live and yawning and falling asleep.

I wanted more, English to me was not about simply learning grammar rules. I was a keen reader and had started reading books in my free time. I loved how words were put together to make interesting stories and paint pictures in my mind. I loved writing I loved the vocabulary and the flow of the English language, why was Mr Toomey not teaching us this.

My salvation from death by boredom came in my second year when a new teacher replaced the old codger Toomey who had retired or was transferred to the residential home for useless teachers.

His replacement was called John Durkin.

John Durkin was a charismatic young teacher from Edinburgh, he had a cosmopolitan outlook, and he dressed in the modern fashionable clothes of the time, Fred Perry shirts, corduroy trousers, hush puppy shoes and a checked sports jacket with the obligatory leather patches on the elbows and had a relaxed but authoritative manner which I admired.

Here was another of the new modern breed of young teachers similar to Claudia Deauville, our beautiful French teacher, who were leading the revolution in education methods, who treated us like human beings and preferred to teach us in a more friendly casual way. I loved this. I remember the first class after he had called the register. The register contained only the surnames and initial of every pupil in the class and had to be checked by every teacher at the beginning of each class to ensure that no one had escaped during the class changeovers. He went around the class asking every boy their first name. He came to me......

"And you...the tall boy at the back"...

This was already a huge improvement...tall... wasn't normally the preferred adjective for most teachers.

"What is your first name?"

"Joseph...sir"

"Joseph eh...I think that is what your mum calls you when she's angry right?"

How did he know that?...when my mum called me Joseph it was usually followed by a few quick slaps...

"JOSEPH!!!...what have I told you about leaving all your books on the table....clear them away NOW!!"...Slappety, slap, slap.

So he continued ..."*What do your friends call you?*"....

"Well Sir...I mean Mr Durkin some call me various names. Big Yin.....Skinny Malinky....Hen Broon...Daddy Long Legs."

The class erupted in howls of laughter......

"But most of my friends call me Joe."

"Fair enough he says ...Joe is what I will call you."

And he did, every time...I loved this, I warmed to him immediately.

He continued to call every boy in the class by first names.

One day when he opened his drawer to get something out I saw a strap, but I never in the two years he taught me saw him use it.

He got angry of course from time to time when he was explaining some point of grammar and some boys would be talking instead of listening.

His chosen method of punishment was to make them stay behind after class and write out some sentences which he would write on the board. This was the first time I had witnessed "detention" being used as a punishment. He wrote each sentence with one grammar or spelling mistake and the boys who were detained had to rewrite the sentences correctly. This punishment was very effective as it made the culprits late for the next class and our following class was P.E.with Jaffa Gilroy.

Being late for Jaffa's class was a major crime and would have been punishable by hanging by the neck until dead if he thought he could get away with it.....

"Honestly your honour, when I entered the gymnasium I was as surprised as the police officer to find the wee boy hanging lifeless from the bars with my belt around his neck...I really have no idea how it happened....I think he might have slipped."......

John Durkin's new form of teaching was a revelation and served to put the troublesome rebels in the class on a friendly footing and succeeded in reducing dramatically the friction between the teacher and pupil.

Teachers like John Durkin were proof of the theory that if a teacher is less formal and intimidating they can still command your respect without resorting to the demoralising verbal and physical abuse of vulnerable young boys. Most teachers at St Patrick's High were psychotic sadists and just didn't understand that all this corporal punishment only served to make the pupils more resentful of them and if teachers and pupils are sworn enemies then communication suffers and this has a serious detrimental effect on their education.

John Durkin introduced me to English literature, poetry and reading books .There were a few of us in the class who admitted to enjoying reading, Me, Graham Woods, Andrew Murray, Donal Curry and Mick McCue.He formed us into a book club and gave us assignments to read specific books, write synopsis of the stories and to meet after school in the school library and talk about and share our opinions of the books and their authors.

Reading opened up a whole new world for me.

"The Lord of the Rings" by JRR Tolkien. "The Old Man of the Sea". By Ernest Hemingway..."The Lord of the Flies" by William Golding were just some of my favourites along with the controversial "Catcher in the Rye by J.D Salinger. Which was banned from our school library but was handed to me one day by John Durkin in a brown paper bag, with a warning that I should never tell any other teacher or adult that he had given it to me or he could lose his job.

One day he asked me to stay behind after class. He told me how happy he was with my progress and that he would like me to read a book and write a synopsis as an assignment for our upcoming English exam.

He handed me a book which would have a major influence on me throughout my life.

I looked at the cover, there was a drawing of a tall skinny man on a horse holding a spear and next to him was a small fat man on a donkey, in the background was a windmill and some distant mountains. The title read "Don Quixote the Man from La Mancha….by Miguel de Cervantes.

I had never heard of this book or its author, but I trusted Mr Durkin's choice and took it home.

From the first sentence, I was hooked….

."In a village of La Mancha, whose name I do not wish to recall, there lived, not very long ago, one of those gentlemen with a lance in the lance-rack, an ancient shield, a skinny old horse, and a fast greyhound."

This first sentence conjured up an immediate picture in my head and had me thirsting for more.

I couldn't put it down, I stuck my head in it at every available minute, and I even read it at the dinner table in my grannies house despite my mum's protestations. It was pure fantasy and I loved it. I read it from cover to cover and back again….

"Would ye put that daft book down and eat yer tea:"

"It's no use talking to him when his face is buried in a book …she continued.

"Leave him alone May"…replied my grannie

"Sure it's better than him running crazy outside, or playing football with all them daft boys from Bontine Avenue."

"It's not a daft book mammy it's called Don Quixote." …….. (I pronounced it kwicksoat)

"And it's about a Spanish nobleman and his servant who travel around Spain having adventures and imaginary fights with windmills and saving people from dragons…...and stuff."

"Acchh it's just filling yer heid with more nonsense….fighting windmills in Spain for god's sake…sure that's the other side of the world…. as if yer not daft enough already."……

My mammy didn't understand……..

This book opened up a whole new world to me and fuelled a burning desire for travel and adventure which has remained with me to this day

I wrote the synopsis, and explained excitedly at the book club, passing it to the other boys for them to read. They weren't as impressed as me.

"Sure it's just a lot of short stories."

"Yes, but it is the way it's written...it's amazing."

"No, I don't agree it's written in old English and too long."

I loved this old English 17th century language translated from 17th century old Spanish.

Nobody got it the way I did.

I reluctantly gave it back to John Durkin a few days later complete with my appraisal.

I got an "A".

When Christmas came around and my mum asked one day what I would like, it was no contest.......

The Adventures of Don Quixote (The Ingenious Gentleman from La Mancha)...by Miguel de Cervantes.

It became my favourite book and I read and re- read it avidly absorbing the exciting, unbelievable stories of fantasy and incredible adventures.

I still have it.

As fate would have it I now live very close to Castilla La Mancha where the mythical Quixote's adventures took place and have visited there many times.

There is a low mountain where they have built replica windmills and although a fictitious mythical character, have statues and even a museum dedicated to Don Quixote and Sancho Panza...

Our school library was very small, the majority of students preferring to play sport. Reading was for sissies.

So in an effort to quench my growing thirst for books I joined the Dumbarton Public Library in Church Street, where I would go at 4.00pm most days after school to borrow some books read them all in a week and return them the following week. Joining the library was my ticket for traveling through time and space. I read poetry books, adventure books, biographies...nothing was out of bounds.

John Durkin was a fantastic teacher and mentor, I never forgot him, and although he didn't know it at the time he was a major influence in my later life. When I was doing my degree in English Language and training to be an English teacher, I often thought of his wise words and now being an English teacher myself, I can only aspire to stimulate my young students' minds as much as he did mine.

Bunking Off (Playing truant)

There weren't too many subjects in school that I hated but one was definitely algebra. It was made up of a lot of incomprehensible squiggles and hieroglyphics like $Ax2 + Bx2$ and $X= Y$ and I really couldn't understand how these obscure equations could possibly be useful to me in the future.

Wee Mr Timony was our algebra teacher and a typical St Pat's teacher who must have been at least 95 years old and well past his sell by date, he was also half blind and deaf, his method of engaging us pupils in the scintillating subject of algebra was to tell us to open our books at a specific page and study the text and complete the exercises whilst he slumped at his desk and had forty winks .To avoid this mind numbing, boring subject I would escape from school leaving someone to answer my name when the teacher called the register...Wee Timony never lifted his gaze from the register, he simply called out the names and if a voice somewhere in the distance answered "present sir" he ticked the name without checking to see who was answering. So it was quite normal practice to bribe another boy to call "present". The favour would be returned when the imposter wanted to avoid his least favourite class.

My schoolmates Chris McKinley and Murt O'Connell also hated this subject and so the Ideal place for us to disappear to during algebra was Chris's father's wood yard.

Chris's dad Colum McKinley was a coalman and had a wood yard near the school where he kept his lorries along with a vast selection of vintage American cars, dogs, chickens and a few goats. I loved going there with Chris his brother Jack and our friends Murt O'Connell and Norman Connolly. We would all disappear to the yard after lunchtime and help his dad with cutting wood, milking the goats, collecting newly laid eggs and any other jobs he would find for us to do and fail to return to school for algebra class. Algebra was our first class after lunch time so we had our lunch then nipped out the back of the school and climbed over the fence and headed for the wood yard.

My mum used to give me 1 shilling a day for my lunch which she expected me to spend on a wholesome school dinner. We had a school canteen where we were served by a gaggle of dinner ladies who had been rejected from the German gestapo selection process for being too cruel. They would stand in line behind huge aluminium containers of what they laughingly called food, holding big, heavy silver ladles which they used to scoop out the daily gruel and slap it on your plate. The daily selection of these culinary masterpieces never changed. it was either steamed white slop, steamed green slop, steamed red slop or on very special occasions steamed yellow slop, all served up by the apathetic ladies with the obligatory burned out fag dangling from their lips, which now and again deposited its unstable residue of ash directly into the slop container. For dessert we had dregs of disgusting semolina with stewed prunes which resembled the pools of vomit I used to see on a Saturday morning in the high street where some drunk had ejected the contents of his stomach the night before.

So the alternative to the school dinner was to go up to Big Ken's shop which was situated opposite the rear school gates.

When I describe Ken's retail emporium as a "shop" I am somewhat over exaggerating and doing a grave disservice to real shops. Ken's shop was more or less a dilapidated concrete shack with a corrugated tin roof which leaked when it rained and served as Big Ken's business enterprise and provided him and all his family with a meagre income. Ken was a man in his late fifties with a mop of wild, grey hair which hadn't seen a comb, brush or shampoo for many years. Judging by his bad attitude he must have suffered some kind of cruel and deprived childhood or perhaps he had been dropped on his head from a great height when he was a baby, whatever the reason it resulted in him despising everyone and only barely tolerating us St Pat's boys because we made up 95 percent of his customers. He always wore the same filthy, old, grey, ripped woollen cardigan with holes in the sleeves and a huge variety of food stains down the front, it was possible to guess from this multi-coloured detritus what he had eaten for lunch and dinner in the previous month just by analysing the stains. His pair of national health glasses, held together with selotape balanced precariously on the end of his spotty, bulbous nose. He always had an abundance of grey stubble on his chin except for the very rare occasions, when he had bothered to shave, his face would then be covered with small pads of tissue paper saturated with blood and green puss where his razor had taken the head off one of his numerous, weeping boils. His long black fingernails had rarely been cut and looked as though he had been digging for coal without the use of a shovel. His crowning glory was the permanent stream of thick, yellow snot dangling from his nose, which he occasionally wiped off with the sleeve of his cardigan or the back of his hand or simply let it drip onto the counter or any nearby uncovered bread or cakes. To complete his professional, shopkeeper look he had, like the dinner ladies, the obligatory woodbine or capstan full strength fag hanging from his drooping lips. What Big Ken lacked in sartorial elegance he made up for with his witty charm and grace.....

"Right ya wee fucking bastards ...whit d'ye want...and be quick a want te shut for ma fucking dinner."

"Half a vee and a packet of cheese and onion Ken....and no snot please."

So I spent my 1 shilling dinner money with Big Ken. Half of a Vienna loaf and a packet of cheese and onion crisps cost 9 pence and made a nutritious and appetizing alternative to the obnoxious slop bucket in the school canteen. I would then remove the dough from inside the loaf and fill it with the crisps, saving some of the dough for later to roll into small balls which would relieve the boredom in maths class by throwing them across the class at one of my classmates. With the extra thrupence I could buy a bag of mixed sweets or three penny caramels whilst most of the other boys chose the alternative desert of a single cigarette. Big Ken, in his endeavours to be named as entrepreneur of the year, would open a packet of 10 cigarettes and sell them individually for 3 pence to any boy who was tall enough to reach the counter. Any small 11 year old who needed a fag simply asked a bigger boy to lift him up so that he could put his thrupence into Ken's grubby, filthy hand and collect his prize of a single woodbine fag which he could then smoke, sitting on the floor next to the overflowing dustbins behind Ken's shop whilst coughing up his lungs, doubled up in pain and gasping for air.

So then off we sauntered to Chris's dad's wood yard.

The yard was at Dalreoch and had a rear entrance which could be accessed from behind our school. It was used by Chris's dad Big Colum McKinley as a storage yard for his coal, wooden logs and the lorries he used for delivering to homes in Dumbarton.

Big Colum was a Dumbarton legend, a huge powerful man 6 foot tall and built like the proverbial brick shithouse...Around the yard were various, rambling outbuildings which stored the wood cutting saws, and dry storage for the coal and wood logs. It also had a selection of other small buildings which housed the various animals. He had goats, chickens, ducks and a selection of vicious dogs which guarded the yard. The dogs were friendly with anyone who was accompanied by Chris or Jack, but I was always very careful to stay close to the boys as I never trusted them. They would come sniffing round my legs, growling and licking their lips while staring at me with a menacing look which said....just wait till we get you alone...nobody will protect you then.

Another activity I enjoyed a lot was milking the goats, Chris taught me how to sit on the stool and wrap my hands around the nanny goats udders and squeeze them in turn to extract the warm milk into a silver bucket.

This had to be done inside the goat shed, which was a long wooden cabin with a door in the middle and a carpet of straw on the floor. I thoroughly enjoyed this milking activity and would lean my head against the nanny goat and reach under and enthusiastically squeeze her udders until I had filled the bucket with fresh, warm goat's milk.

This particular nanny had a jealous mate. A vicious, aggressive billy which Chris had nicknamed "Wild Bill" and who took great offence to anyone touching his wife's titties and so to ensure the safety of the milker, he had to be tied up securely at the other end of the shed to allow the daily milking to take place.

So one day Chris asked me to milk the nanny which he knew I loved...I collected the stool and the bucket and made for the goat shed.........

"Don't forget to tie up Wild Bill Joe ...you know how possessive he is about his nanny"

"Aye nae bother Chris"...

So with Chris's warning ringing in my ears I collected the Wild Bill and tied him up securely with a few double knots at the other end of the shed whilst I set about enthusiastically milking his nanny.

I was lost in the moment and busy squishing and squeezing and leaning my head on the nanny when suddenly I heard a rumbling noise which I thought was thunder. I turned around and there was Wild Bill only a couple of feet away and heading at full speed straight for me, head down and snorting wildly and he was obviously not happy. His horns made contact with my bottom and sent me flying off the stool onto the floor. I crawled through the straw into the corner and trembling with fear I tried to compose myself. He had me cornered and was standing glaring at me and preparing for the next charge. As my only escape route was now blocked I called out for help from Chris.., no reply....Jack. No reply...Colum...no reply...

Oh my god I thought 'I'm on my own and they are busy in another part of the yard and can't hear me shouting...... I'm going to die.

I tried to make myself inconspicuous and was quietly talking to the billy and assuring him that I had definitely no romantic inclinations towards his nanny and I was merely touching her titties to extract the milk. Billy was having none of my explanations and charged again. With the skills of a top Spanish bullfighter I side stepped him and as he ran past me and collided with the wall. I took advantage of the situation and made a bolt for the door at full speed. I raced outside and there standing outside the door was Chris, Jack and Big Colum convulsed in fits of laughter with tears running down their faces.

"What the fuck happened Joe? I told you to tie the billy up" ...said Chris when he finally recovered from his laughing fit.

*."I did Chris...I did.....I'm sure I did.... I don't know how he got loose"....*I replied breathlessly whilst shaking like a leaf.

Only later did I discover that Jack had sneaked into the shed while I was busy and lost in the milking moment and he had untied the billy then sneaked out again.

So my escape from the charging Wild Bill was just one big joke for the Mckinleys to be recounted later on many occasions in school and no doubt during McKinley family gatherings.

Chris and Jack were big, strong boys. Their father had them lifting bags of coal and helping him on his coal delivery rounds since they were small children. Loading coal on the lorry for them was easy. While I struggled with both hands to drag a coal sack a couple of inches along the floor they simply hoisted one straight onto their backs in one smooth movement and threw it onto the lorry.

Cutting logs with the circular saw was another activity which scared me.

Particularly after I witnessed Jack having his finger sliced off by the electric sawing machine.

Jack and Chris were always fighting. They were both strong and fit so these fights would be toe to toe stuff with punches flying into each other's swollen, bloody faces, followed by wrestling each other to the floor and rolling around screaming obscenities. They usually ended after half an hour or so in a draw with both shaking hands and making friends again.

This fight was different. Jack was in the woodshed cutting logs using the electric circular saw and for some unknown reason Chris went in and punched him on the back of the head. In the ensuing scuffle Jack stumbled and to regain his balance put out his hand onto the saw bench, another punch from Chris resulted in his hand slipping and making contact with the spinning saw blade and his finger flying into the air having been severed by the saw.

Well Jack was obviously shocked and in pain and screamed for his dad.

Big Colum rushed into the shed and observed the situation......

"What the fuck is going on?"

*"Erm...... Jack fell onto the saw and had wee accident".......*said Chris

With blood now spurting out of the gap where his finger used to be Jack just screamed hysterically......

"Ach away ya wee sissy"...said Big Colum

"Sure it's only a finger...yer lucky it wisnae yer whole hand"

He picked of an old oily rag off the floor, shook it to remove the sawdust and wrapped it around Jack's hand......

"Now you two carry on loading the logs onto the lorry and when we finish the rounds I'll take you to the cottage hospital for a couple of stitches....yell be fine, sure you've got another nine fingers.

So off they went on the coal delivery rounds as if having a finger cut off by an electric saw was a normal everyday occurrence.......The dogs fought over the tasty morsel of Jack's juicy, severed finger..... and me, Murt and Norman trudged back to school.

Gigs, Bogeys…...and other transport

In the 50's and 60's when I was a child hardly anyone except the very rich people had cars.

The streets were empty and we children could play safely on almost any street without any threat of danger. When a car did appear we simply stopped our game and moved out of the way, only to resume our positions after it passed. This evasive action was repeated every half hour or so when a car would pass slowly along the street. We could cycle along the middle of any road in complete safety and every street and road was considered to be our playground.

We built gigs and bogeys made from old planks of wood, wooden boxes and pram wheels.

We were very competitive and would have gig races around the streets of Brucehill, careering down the hill from Caledonia Terrace to Firth View and praying that when we reached the main road there weren't any cars passing at the same time, then flying straight across the road and only stopping when we collided with the bushes at the bottom throwing everyone on the ground with the gig on top.

I was lucky, when my dad was working as a bin man he was under my strict instructions to collect any old prams he found at the rubbish tip and bring them home for me to work my magic. So I always had a constant supply of spare wheels and planks as replacements when one gig was destroyed, I simply built a new one.

The basic design of a gig was a thick plank of wood resting on top of two sets of pram wheels. However, go-faster extras could be added such as wooden boxes, old milk crates, or anything we found on the shore or in the streets that would make it more aero dynamic and enhance the performance and the looks. These accessories were simply attached to the plank using six inch nails which .being too long were then bent over to secure the additional body parts. There were no brakes of course and so traveling at break neck speed down hills I needed to put my feet on the ground to stop the gig., thus encountering the wrath of my irate mother who, when I returned home for tea, would offer me some gentle, parental advice about the dangers of downhill speeding…...............

"Come here ya wee tinker"….slappety. slap. slap

"Would ye look at the state of them shoes"…slappety. slap. slap

"Whit did I tell ye about using yer feet to stop that stupid gig", slappety.., slap.., slap

"If I see you doing that again I'll take a hatchet to that gig", slappety. slap..,slap.

"Aye OK mammy….no need to keep on ".

I couldn't understand my mammy….an out of control, speeding gig was a danger to innocent people who might inadvertently cross my trajectory. The absence of brakes and steering control, to avoid hitting these pedestrians, meant that I had no option but to scrape my feet along the ground, thus slowing or stopping the speeding gig and avoiding colliding with and injuring or even killing the poor pedestrian, she should have been proud of me…........me and my scuffed shoes were saving lives.

Of course the parental advice was ignored and the warning forgotten as five minutes later after teatime, once again with shoes grinding on the tarmac the gig was careering out of control downhill.

I loved building gigs and put a great deal of thought and effort into the design and construction. The gig usually only lasted a few days as it was never built to withstand the abuse it received, sometimes carrying three or four boys, with another pushing at breakneck speed along a flat road, when the gig reached a suitable speed the pusher jumped on too, or speeding downhill with all five on board. With all this weight the axles, which were only designed to take the weight of a pedigree pram and small baby would simply break or bend at 45 degrees, or the odd wheel would fly off whilst traveling at high speed or the plank snap in two, thus rendering the gig a useless wreck.

Back to the drawing board and within a few days another new, stronger gig was built

If we were short of wheels and planks we just built wheelbarrows, which we called "bogeys" only one set of wheels and a wooden box was required for this particular vehicle of fun. It could be pushed by one boy with a long wooden pole with the other sitting snugly inside the box.

We had races and competitions where we steered slalom fashion between dustbins placed at intervals in the middle of the road.

We would take our gigs and wheelbarrows to the cliff in Brucehill where we could freewheel down the cliff face or to the monument in Castle hill and let the gig pick up speed down one hill and momentum take it to the top of the other and see who could stay upright the longest or reach the bottom fastest.

Crashing and turning over was a common occurrence and at the end of the day we would trudge home, pulling our gigs with a length of clothes rope, "borrowed" from our mum's washing line and with various war wounds and blood streaming from our faces, arms and legs. I still have to this day the souvenir scars caused by overturning, colliding and crashing during our very own versions of formula one meets wacky races.

Our next door neighbour in Carrick terrace was a man called Jerry Boyle. Jerry was a milkman with the co-op dairies and would start work early in the morning and finish around lunchtime.

Now Jerry had a motorbike. A big, red shiny monster BSA which he loved. He used to park it outside our house and when he started it up the noise was both frightening and thrilling.

He would spend hours cleaning and polishing it a couple of times a week.

When it was parked outside and Jerry was sleeping in the afternoon I would just sit on the pavement next to it or walk around it examining in awe all of the shiny metal bits connected by random cables and wires and tubes. I was amazed and intrigued how such a machine with two wheels and no pedals could move and keep balanced.

It had two seats and if I stood on tiptoes I could just about touch the handlebars.

I looked at my reflexion on the curved, highly polished chrome and made faces at myself in the round mirrors. I drew wee faces in the puddle of oil underneath and wrote my name on the pavement with my oily fingers.

I was fascinated by this motorbike I sat for hours trying to figure out how it worked how could it move? how could it stop? And why didn't it fall over like my wee bicycle. I had watched fascinated while Jerry kicked and jumped on something at the side when suddenly with an almighty roar the engine sprang to life. He then sat on the seat put his hands on the handlebars, did what looked like a wee dance with his feet and hands touching and pulling and pushing levers and pedals then he was off in a cloud of smoke down the street. I was left open mouthed.

When I heard Jerry arriving outside the house I was always excited and would ask my mum if I could go out and watch Jerry cleaning his bike.

My biggest thrill arrived one day while I was sitting in my usual position on the pavement next to this goddess when Jerry appeared. I watched as he started cleaning and polishing, rubbing and wiping when suddenly he asked me if I wanted to help him.

What?' would I help? This request to me was like an invitation to a child to go into a sweet shop and help themselves. He gave me a wee cloth and demonstrated what I should do…….

"Take the cloth and rub this shiny bit here …this is called the gearbox, but be careful not to touch the chain with the clean cloth"

This was the first time I had ever touched the motorbike with Jerry's full permission and I was in heaven, then followed a full detailed description by Jerry of every part of the bike.

"Do you see this bit here …well that's the brake …that makes it stop."

"And this lever here is called the kick start …this make the engine start."

I had a million questions to ask and Jerry was very patient and did his best to answer every one.

"What's this lever for?"

"Well that's the front brake you pull it and the wheel stops going round".

"And this? What's this cable?"

"That's called the clutch. You squeeze it to change the gears."

"What's the gears?"

This education was fascinating. Why didn't the teachers in school teach me interesting stuff like this instead of the boring maths lessons?

This cleaning ritual continued sometimes for hours and I would follow Jerry's instructions and absorb all the information while he told me his stories about his adventures on his motorbike.

I was hooked.

I asked my mum when I could have a motorbike like Jerry's

"Ach away and don't be silly, sure yer just a wean."

It would be another 10 years before I realized my dream.

I was 16 and working as an apprentice painter and decorator with H Waddle and Son in Helensburgh.

I had to start work at 8.00am and started off by catching the SMT bus on the Cardross Rd every morning at 7.15. Sitting every morning on the overcrowded, freezing, smelly old bus for 45 minutes and breathing in the pungent cigarette smoke of all the other passengers was agony for me.

I figured I urgently needed an alternative form of transport.

My salvation came from a friend called Puggy Peters who also worked in Helensburgh and as he also started at 8.00 am he offered to give me a lift each day on his scooter. All I had to do was to be at the bottom of Brucehill at 7.30am and as we both finished at the same time he would give me a lift home too of course I should share the petrol expenses.

Puggy's personal choice of transport was a scooter, a shiny, red Lambretta SX200 I loved this scooter. The freedom, the wind in my face, the vibration and the sound of the engine, the smell of the two stroke exhaust and after a week of getting a lift each day on this dream machine I was hooked .I decided that I must have my own scooter.

I talked about it to my parents and although my mum was hesitant, as she considered scooters and motorbikes to be dangerous. She pointed out all my scars from crashing my gigs and said that if I couldn't control a four wheel vehicle then she had serious doubts about my ability to remain upright on two wheels. I reassured her and explained that the scooter had real, working brakes and that I wouldn't wear out more pairs of shoes and that I would be careful and ride slowly and I could pay weekly with my own money from my meagre wages.

So eventually she relented and gave her permission......

The day came when my dad took me to Glasgow's Gallowgate area near to Glasgow cross where there was a garage which sold second hand scooters.

My choice was a white Vespa GS 160 only two years old and with very low mileage, it was very basic but the garage agreed to throw in a windshield and a front luggage rack. It cost 150 pounds.

As I was only 16 my dad signed the credit agreement, I would pay 7 pounds a month for 2 years...

I had my scooter...I was so excited. The next week my dad borrowed a van from my mum's cousin Frankie Bell and me, my dad and my sister travelled to Glasgow and collected my scooter. I had never ridden a scooter before but after being a pillion passenger every day and watching Puggy ridding his and remembering Jerry Boyle's detailed instructions years before I knew I would have no problem .Back home in Caledonia Terrace outside my Grannie Gows house was a crescent with an empty road. I practiced until I had the knack of riding changing gears and stopping. I stuck on some "L" plates and I was off. My Grannie Gow decided that she should have the honour of being the first to ride on the passenger seat .So, although illegal, off we went whizzing around the crescent, with my grannie waving to all the neighbours who had gathered at their gates to witness the amazing spectacle of grannie Gow on the back of a scooter.

"Are you OK grannie?" I shouted above the noise of the engine

"Sure son, it's fantastic"...she screeched

"This is the biggest thrill I've had between my legs for years"

"Round again...round again."

We must have done at least 10 circuits before my mum and aunties persuaded her that enough was enough.

"Oh that was smashing son...that's the best fun I've had for ages."

I used it every day to travel to and from Helensburgh to work, through rain, hail, snow and storms. I bought some fancy, chrome mirrors and accessories for the scooter, an American army surplus parka coat with a fur collar, gloves and a tartan scarf for me.Now I could spend weekends with Puggy and my other scooter friends, Bobby Murphy ,Peter Deeny, Tom Robinson. We were the top acne ridden mods in Dumbarton.

An added advantage, I soon happily discovered was that despite the acne I was now very popular with girls who all wanted to ride on the back.

Of course it was illegal to take pillion passenger whilst still a learner.

So when I had the opportunity to pick up a girl I simply took off the L plates...surely I would never be stopped by the police.........

Wrong.........

One Sunday we arranged to meet up with our friends the mods from Helensburgh and set off in convoy for a visit to The Barras in Glasgow, So there were about fifteen of us roaring down Sauchiehall Street in Glasgow showing off and with a girl on the pillion seat each, suddenly there at the end of the street appeared two big Glasgow coppers with their hands out.

To say I was nervous is an understatement......

"Hello boys ...where are all you boys going on your wee shiny, fancy scooters?"

"Up to the Barras sir."

(We all called policemen sir in those days)

"Aye and I suppose ye have all got your licences and documents for them wee hairdryers."

"Sure sir."

He went around scrutinising all the licences.

He came to me...I tried to act calm.

He looked at my licence

"Son ...this is a provisional licence."

"A provisional licence means you are a learner."

"EEErrrmm no sir...I mean yyyess sir...I mean noooo sir."

"Well which is it son?"

I decided through a mixture of bravado and optimism to lie........

"Weell yeess the licence is provisional but I passed my test two weeks ago and haven't changed my licence yet."

"OH he says...so you HAVE passed your test then?"

I was shaking now....

"Yes sir...I stammered."

"Two weeks ago eh?"

"Yes sir."

"Open your cubby box son."

I opened the box and inside were my L plates where I had stuffed them just before I picked up the girl…

"Aaahhhhh….so let me get this straight son…you passed your test two weeks ago and instead of ripping up and throwing away the L plates….like most normal people do….you decided to keep them as souvenirs inside your cubby box…is this correct."

He wrote down my name address and licence number…

"I will be checking on these facts as soon as I get back to the station."

He moved his face closer to mine, narrowed his eyes and gave me a cold look.

"And if you're lying to me sonny boy…an officer of the law…you are going to be in big trouble….do you understand?"

"Yes sir….honest sir…… I'm not lying."

Right you wee boys get on your way and don't be breaking any speed limits on them wee scooters."

I was in agony for a couple of weeks whilst at any moment expecting a knock on the door from a big policeman who would slap me in handcuffs and throw me in the van and haul me off to prison for taking a passenger without a full licence AND for lying to a police officer……the knock never came.

I decided I had to pass my test……

Friday 14th April was the date, I had read the highway code many times and annoyed my sister by making her ask me random questions and so I was confident I would pass the test.

All went well, I remembered to look over my shoulder before giving hand signals and on Station Road successfully completed an emergency stop and kept my balance.

The examiner walked along the pavement beside me and told me to ride alongside at the same pace as him.

I hadn't bargained for this and didn't prepare for it.I started off and before I realized it I was about 20 yards ahead of him. He called me back…

"Did you fully understand my instructions son?"

"Erm no not exactly"

"OK I will give you the benefit of the doubt and let you do it again."

"Now this time ride next to the pavement at walking pace alongside me."

This time, mission accomplished and after a few questions about the Highway Code, he handed me my pass slip.

I took off the L plates, ripped them up and threw them in the bin….like most normal people do.

I spent my weekends cleaning, polishing and looking after my pride and joy

My curiosity got the better of me so one snowy, winter weekend when I was bored and I couldn't ride my scooter I decided to discover how the two stroke engine worked. I removed the engine and much to my mum's horror, took it into the kitchen and dismantled it on the floor. I cleaned every part and put it all back together again.

Another weekend I painted it red with gold stripes and with my name in gold letters and with the red white and blue target symbol on the front.

I completely customized it with all the accessories I could afford

I loved my scooter and enjoyed many happy adventures, romantic and otherwise with it.

I figured that with two wheels I was very popular with the girls so surely it follows logically that if I was on four wheels my success would double.

I was 17 on December 24th 1968 and decided I must have a car.

I needed to pass my driving test but as far as I was concerned that was just a formality.

My Dad had taught me to drive when I was a small child. He was a delivery driver for Mason's furniture shop and then he was a driver with Dumbarton County Council, he drove the bin lorries. When I was 8 years old he would take me in his Mason's van and sit me on his knee, he would operate the pedals and he let me put my hands on the steering wheel so that I could steer the van. Later when I was 11 or 12 he was driving the bin lorries and my feet could reach the pedals he showed me how to operate the clutch, brakes and accelerator. I would sometimes go with him on his collection rounds during the school holidays and when we arrived at the rubbish dump we swapped places and I drove the lorry and reversed to the tipping spot and even operated the hydraulic tipping mechanism.

These were my driving lessons, and now that I had passed my motorbike test and I knew the Highway Code all that was left to do was to apply for my test. My date arrived it was to be on the 17th February 1969 5 weeks after my 17th birthday. My dad had a consul 375 with a bench seat and column change gearshift and at weekends he would put on the L plates and come out with me to give me some advice and for me to practice all the manoeuvres I would need to perfect for the test.

I awoke excited on the 17th ready to do my test, but as I opened my bedroom curtains my heart sank, it had been snowing and the ground was covered in frozen glistening snow. I went out to the phone box and called the test centre.

"Hello….. I have a driving test at 11.00 this morning and am calling to find out if the test is cancelled and when is the next available date."

"Why would you assume the test is cancelled?"

"Eeerrrmmm…well…because of the snow."

"Well Joseph….. If you will be driving a car in Scotland then you need to be able to drive in freezing conditions…so be here at 11.00 am sharp."

Risk street was the test centre, and as I registered another blow. My examiner was a woman. This woman had the reputation of being very strict and very few people passed with her first time.

So we set off driving around the town, she tested my reversing ability, next the hill start. Then as we turned into Crosslet Road she informed me that somewhere along this road she would slap the dashboard. This was the signal for me to carry out an emergency stop.

"You must stop the car in full control and with the engine running."

I was ready…SLAP….brakes with clutch and suddenly we were spinning after completing 360deg res the car stopped and with my foot still on the clutch the engine was still running. What she hadn't bargained for was the black ice on the road under the frozen snow.

Through 25% skill and 75% luck I controlled the skidding car without touching the kerb and ended up facing in the right direction. I glanced at the examiner and noticed her hands were gripping the dashboard and her face was white.

"I don't think I will ask you to do that again" she said

I figured that now I had surely failed and I completely relaxed. We continued with the test route and I carried out a perfect three point turn.

By the time we arrived back at the test centre the snow was falling heavily.

She asked me some Highway Code questions...then to my surprise told me that I had passed.

"Excuse me for asking but what about the skid on the ice on Crosslet Road.?"

*"Well "*she said *"I was very impressed with your ability to control the car on ice ...and decided in the interests of road safety not to ask you to repeat it."*

Now it was blowing a blizzard and I heard that all the following tests for that day were cancelled due to black ice and treacherous conditions.

So now I had my car driving licence and the use of my dad's Ford Consul whenever he didn't need it.

Some weekends my dad used the car to take my mum shopping or to the Dixon Bowling Club and I had to go back on two wheels again.

The problem was that now I was used to the convenience and comfort of having my own passion wagon I was losing interest in getting wet and frozen riding my scooter and at 6ft 2in I was having to sit so far back on the pillion seat because of my long legs I decided it was time to make the change to a car permanently.

So I sold my beloved Vespa scooter and bought myself a Ford Prefect.

I had seen it sitting outside a garage in Clydebank for sale and fell in love with it immediately.

It was black with brown seats, a three speed gearbox and a wee 800 cc engine....AND most important...it had a radio.

Although not as comfortable as the Consul we still managed to squeeze 6 people in when we went out on weekends.

Saturday nights we all piled into the car and headed for Duck Bay Marina.

Duck Bay Marina was the popular place to go to pick up girls. It had the advantage of being quite remote, on the banks of Loch Lomond about 5 miles from Balloch and was a fantastic Saturday night music venue but you needed a car. Lots of the local girls went there by bus from Balloch and the last bus back was about 9.00pm way too early, the night was just starting, so they were very interested in anyone who could give them a lift home. I never considered myself to be the most handsome teenager in Dumbarton, but now at 17 and bursting with self-confidence, my acne under control, experienced in the "front bum" action...AND....I had a car.

We would go to Casci's on Saturday afternoons and put the word out that we would be in the Duck Bay Marina that night and that a lift home might be available for certain girls in return for certain favours...my friend Mick Casey was more direct....

"Right girls who wants a lift back from the Marina tonight? Cock it, or walk it"...he would tell them flashing his cheeky smile.

Mick had a real way with words......

Front Bums and Dangly Bits

I was about 7 years old when I discovered that wee girls were physically different from us wee boys....

We lived in Carrick Terrace in Castlehill. Me and my big sister, Marie Therese had some friends across the road. The Gren family, Paul Victor and Ellen were the children. Paul was my age and Victor a year or so younger. Ellen was the same age as my sister three years older than me.We used to play with them after school and at weekends. Children's games in the streets were Hide and Seek, Tag, Kick the Can, Hopscotch, Skipping Ropes, or we just invented any activity which we found entertaining. Everything we needed for fun was right outside our doors. We didn't have televisions, computers, and internet or play stations so we just let our vivid imaginations run wild. When it rained or was too cold we played in each other's houses usually staying for tea and returning home when it was dark...

One rainy day we were in the Gren's house upstairs in the bedroom playing doctors and nurses. This was a boring game for us boys, we preferred playing Cowboys and Indians or any game which involved fighting and killing, so this was a girl's game and we boys were forced to join in as the script required some male doctors. My sister and Ellen were happy inventing stories of hospital patients having their lives saved by handsome doctors. So me and Paul and Victor had to act the roles of the hero doctors and Marie Therese was the nurse and Ellen had the role of the dying patient. The deathbed scene required Ellen to lie face down on the bed whilst the doctor examined her to diagnose her life threatening illness....

"Mmmmm nurse...pass me the knife I think I will have to operate."

"Please be careful doctor don't cut her skin, she will bleed and she will die."

"Don't worry nurse I am a doctor ...I know what to do."

"Oohhh doctor you're so brave and handsome.

"Now Ellen lift up your vest please and take down your knickers."

There was a lot of laughing and giggling from my sister and Paul and Victor and

Ellen was acting the part with the enthusiasm and skill of a Hollywood actress. She lifted up her vest and as I was pretending to operate on her back, she slipped down her navy blue knickers and exposed her bare bum, more laughing and giggling and then suddenly she turned over onto her back and what a shock I had......

Ellen Gren had two bums! A small one at the front and a bigger one at the back..... What a revelation. There was a distinct lack of dangly bits at the front like mine.

I had never noticed this abnormality before when I shared a bedroom with my sister and also a tin bath in front of the fire on Friday nights in our old house in Clyde Street. I was too young to notice any differences and was too busy avoiding the wooden scrubbing brush and screaming when the carbolic soap that my mum used to wash us splashed into my eyes.

There was a lot of giggling from the girls and stunned silence from me and her brothers who, I presume were just as shocked as I was to see their sister's bare arse.

I think that was the defining moment when I became interested in girls. They couldn't kick a ball, run, climb trees or steer a gig, but my god this two bum trick was a sure-fire winner in my book.

From that moment on I saw girls in a different light and was continually trying to satisfy my innocent curiosity by asking wee girls in the streets to show me their two bums.

My first girlfriend when we lived in Brucehill was Catherine Casey, well when I say girlfriend, I really mean that she was the first girl I kissed. We were 9 or 10 years old and were never officially a couple however, it was generally accepted among our group of friends that we were destined to be married, have 6 children and to live happily ever after. The Caseys were a big family who lived in the same street as us in Caledonia Terrace and like all children were always playing outside together. Catherine was around my age and in my youthful opinion was the most beautiful girl I had ever seen....more beautiful than that actress Marilyn Monroe....I was smitten.

We used to play with all the other children on the swings and down at the bushes on the wasteland in Firth View Terrace at the top of the cliff and me and Catherine would escape from the crowds, run off hand in hand and find a nice quiet bush to hide behind and practice our film star kisses. This activity involved putting our lips together, mouths closed of course and moving our heads from side to side like we had seen at the pictures when a cowboy kissed a cowgirl and all the children would shout woooohoooo.

So me and Catherine perfected our technique until we could hold the kiss for about 15-20 minutes, all the time breathing through our noses, a side effect of this activity was the curtain of snott which accumulated around the chin and nose and which periodically had to be wiped away with a mucky hand to avoid drowning.

As children we didn't really understand much about the rituals of boyfriends and girlfriends, we were usually matched up by other kids during games like kiss-n-chase where us boys would chase a girl we liked until we caught her and claim the prize of a kiss. If the girl liked you then you were rewarded with a peck on the cheeks or if you were lucky.... the lips.

"Joe's got a girlfriend...

"Joe's got a girlfriend"

"na na na na na "

Later this changed to.....

"She loves you....... yeah yeah yeah."

"She loves you ....yeah yeah yeah yeah."

If she didn't like you it was a punch on the mouth, and as some Brucehill girls were bigger and tougher than us wee boys you had better be sure of your chances before you caught her or you would go home crying to your mum with a black eye and a fat lip.

We went to birthday parties where we played innocent games like "round goes the bun". This game involved all the girls sitting on the floor on cushions and the boys, with a cushion in his hands walking around the circle of girls, choosing one he licked and kneeling in front of her and kissing her on the lips, to loud cheers and laughter from all the others at the party.........

Round goes the bun

The jolly old bun

Round goes the bun once more

He kneels to the prettiest girl in the room

And kisses her on the fl-o-o-o-r……..

As we got older this game developed into kissing in the privacy of a dark cupboard.

This closed mouth kissing was all we knew. I personally never graduated to the new open mouth, with tongues, technique until I was a teenager.

When I was in secondary school having a girlfriend was obligatory.

Let me add that these early teen girlfriends were what we would call these days *"virtual"* girlfriends.

Quite different from the actual *"virtual"* girlfriends I had in my dad's *"men only"* magazines.

Our school St Patrick's in Castlehill was an all-boys school and the girls went to Notre Dame High school for girls where they were taught by nuns and was situated in a convent near to Brucehill.

Due to some catastrophic error by some unthinking adult both schools ended at the same time in the afternoon…. 4 o clock.

Hundreds of pubescent, horny boys and girls emerged into the daylight and mixed together at the bottom of Brucehill.

We all hung around outside Hart's sweetie shop and the Co-op shop at the bottom of Brucehill. Away from the control of teachers and parents, this was a no man's land of freedom and rebellion. Groups of boys on one side of the road and girls on the other with the boys all shouting and showing off and the girls giggling in appreciation. Across the road from the shops was a triangle of grass with a big flagpole in the middle which, with our ingenious, inventive imagination we called the "Flaggy". This was our meeting point for watching the girls and also where the regular after school fight club gathered. The fights were an almost daily occurrence and so when the fights started all the boys would form a big circle to cheer on their chosen gladiator, with the girls looking on, screaming and with their hands over their mouths. I wasn't interested in the fights and preferred to take this opportunity to eye up the girls. If I saw one I fancied I would simply get a friend to go over and ask one of her friends to ask her if she would go out with me or give him a wee hand written note to pass on…….

"D'ye want tae go out with me?"

If the answer came back yes…then I had a girlfriend. This form of communication saved the sender the acute embarrassment of facing personal rejection if the girl didn't fancy him and said no. The alternative was to cross the road and speak to a girl face to face and this was just too scary to contemplate. If you did this and were rejected…. it was a very long walk back across the road to your mates who were all waiting to jeer and ridicule you relentlessly. We never talked to, or met these "virtual" girlfriends, we never actually went on dates, it was just accepted as official that if the answer was yes then you had a girlfriend. Until two weeks later when her friend would tell your friend to tell you or send a note to tell you that you were chucked and so the passionate love affair would end as quickly as it had begun.

I remember one such occasion when I really fancied a girl who I had seen every day outside Hart's. I sent my friend John White across to find out her name. She was called Marie Bridges I hadn't seen her around Dumbarton so I guessed she was from out of town. It transpired that she was from Haldane in Balloch. This was bad news because if the Balloch boys discovered I had a "virtual" girlfriend from Balloch I would get a good kicking and that would definitely not be virtual. She was a stunner, long dark hair and a straight fringe which almost covered her eyes. I thought that she was gorgeous and at that moment my love knew no bounds or barriers so I threw caution to the wind and figured that with my ability to outrun most boys in school I would take the risk.

We exchanged our vows through mutual friends as usual and the big romance started. She was so excited about her new virtual lover that she told all her Balloch friends on the bus home that she had a new boyfriend called Joe Mcloughlin. What she overlooked was the fact that on the same bus where she announced this momentous event were all of the Balloch boys from my school who overheard the news.

The next day in school in our P.E. class we were doing the usual circuit training, running around the gym in circles, when I felt a sudden whack on the back of my head. At first I thought it was our teacher Jack Gilroy giving me his customary welcome greeting .I turned round and came face to face with Mick Law. A fearsome Balloch boy...and well known bully.

He grabbed me round the neck in a strangle hold and forced me to the floor where he launched a vicious assault on my face with his fists, quickly joined by other balloch boys who, seeing Mick taking me down and like a pack of hungry lions they wanted to join in the kill and administered multiple kicks to my ribs.

"You ya bastard d'ye think you can steal one of our girls eh?"

Slap.... punch.... pummel

"What are you talking about?" ......I managed to squeak.

"You ya big useless, skinny shite... going out with Marie Bridges."

"Mmme...mmmeee? no!, no!.. I'm not going out with her...she asked me to go out with her.".... I stuttered ..."but I refused because I knew she was yours and from Balloch."*

I tried to get myself out of trouble by lying and at the same time attempted to protect my face.....the face which was now in the process of being used as a punch bag.

Luckily, I was saved by the bell so to speak.

The bell for the end of the period sounded and Jaffa appeared from his office where he had been busy drinking tea and reading the sports pages in the Daily Record.

"What is going on here in my gym?"........"Mcloughlin ya lang streak of misery get up off the floor."*

As I staggered to my feet Mick law got in another wee sly punch to my stomach and whispered in my ear....

"See you in the flaggy at 4 o'clock...ya bastard."

Oh my god this was terrifying.... .I was going to be killed

I was petrified.

The news quickly spread around the school......

"Mcloughlin is going to fight at 4 .o'clock in the flaggy."

"Which Mcloughlin?"

"Joe Mcloughlin"

"Whit!!!!.....Joe Mcloughlin that big skinny malinky long legs from Brucehill?"

"Aye! that's him:"

"But he's a big Jessie...He couldn't fight his way out of a paper bag"

"Who is he fighting?"

"Mick Law."

"What??..Mick "psycho killer" Law from Balloch?"

"Aye. That's right."

"He's going to die."

"This we've got to see"

"Bwahahahahahahaha!!!"

This wasn't just going to be the fight of the decade but rather the slaughter of the century....it was David and Goliath in the Flaggy.

I considered my options....I could run away, leave town.....or better still, leave the country....I could jump in front of the Brucehill bus, suffering considerably less injuries than I was certain to suffer at the hands of Mick Law......I could go directly to the hospital and sign myself in to save the ambulance the bother of taking me there...I could run home at 4 o'clock and ask my grannie to come down to the flaggy and fight Mick Law with her walking stick instead of me.

Or I could put on a brave face and show up at the flaggy with my supporters......

Oh wait a minute.......... I didn't have any supporters because all my cowardly, so called friends were more scared of Mick Law than me and as soon as they heard the news about the forthcoming combat, cancelled our friendship, quickly changed their names to Judas and abandoned me to my fate.

There was no escape.......

After careful consideration I decided that my best and possibly my only chance of survival would be to stand in front of him, arms by my side and let him use me as a punchbag.I would stand like a statue and offer no resistance whatsoever. I figured it would only take two or three punches and be all over in minute. I wouldn't cry, plead for mercy or cry for my mum. I would simply not put up a fight. I would collapse on the floor, bloodied and defeated. All Mick's friends would carry their conquering hero off to the bus stop on their shoulders and I would be left lying in the Flaggy ,maybe for days, until someone had the courage to come out of the shadows. Collect my lifeless, bloodied body and take me home and explain to my mum that her son died a hero in a battle over the honour of a beautiful girl called Marie Bridges.

I was delighted with my master plan. I rationalised that this ingenious tactic could indeed save my life. I might end up with facial disfigurement and be confined to a wheelchair and be fed through a tube for the rest of my life....but by god I would still be alive.

It was four o'clock. I was ready...I had been exercising my facial muscles all afternoon in a forlorn attempt to toughen them up to withstand the forthcoming onslaught that was about to happen in the flaggy.

This fight drew the biggest crowd of the year. It was standing room only.... boys and girls from Brucehill, Castlehill and Westcliffe and of course Balloch. I put my school bag on the ground, we both took off our school blazers I rolled up my shirt sleeves in an effort to look tough and prepared for combat.

We stood face to face. He started dancing around and showing off his fancy footwork by doing the "Ali Shuffle" whilst I stood motionless, frozen to the spot with fear and with my arms by my side. Then suddenly he lunged at me with fists flying, to my surprise my well thought out plan failed he had caught me off guard. I dodged the first punch with lightning fast reflexes, I dodged the second and the third, and he couldn't land a punch. I realized I had an undiscovered talent to move my head out of the way a split second before his fist was due to connect with my face.

He was getting frustrated....

"Stand still ya big skinny bastard...I'm going to kill ye"....he shrieked

The crowd was baying for blood. They came here to see a fight and this performance from these two gladiators was just not satisfying enough.

Suddenly and without warning, I honestly don't know where it came from, as he was off balance I grabbed him in a sort of clumsy bear hug. I had watched Mick McManus on the T.V. wrestling on a Saturday afternoon use this move to immobilise Jackie Pallo and it worked for him. So by my reckoning if I wrapped my long arms around him and clasped my hands round his back and pinned his arms by his side he would be unable to punch me. He tried to head-butt me at point blank range, but again I moved my head out of the way. We stumbled around then fell to the ground still in this bear hug and rolled over a couple of times. As fate would have it we landed with him lying on the floor face up and me straddling on top with my legs pinning down his shoulders. I seized the moment and I started pummelling his face with my fists. I was not a strong boy and although the punches were feeble and weak I surprised myself by connecting with my target with each wild punch. His face was turning red and his nose began to bleed. Sensing the remote possibility of me not actually dying, I closed my eyes and rained multiple punches on him with every ounce of strength I possessed.

"Stop! Stop!!...I give in...I give in."...he pleaded

Now in those days of honour between enemies when one boy gave in that meant that the other had won....and the fight stopped.

My new group of adoring fans cheered their conquering hero.

I was unsure, but gave him the benefit of the doubt and got off. He stood up and took a step back, holding his bloody face in his hands, then flew at me again.

My friend Andy Dobbin who was my next door neighbour, older and who had been a spectator now seeing this injustice jumped on him and grabbed him round the neck and punched him to the floor.

On witnessing this intervention all the Balloch boys then jumped on Andy. This was the signal that now that the one to one fight was officially over then it was open house and so all the Brucehill boys joined in too It was like a scene from the wild west films we watched regularly in the Regal cinema.

Realizing they were hopelessly outnumbered the Balloch boys gave in, collected their wounded hero and friends and ran off to the bus stop.

I had not only won a fight for the first time in my life, but moreover, a fight against Mick Law. I was elated. I was declared a hero. To the hero the spoils...now Marie Bridges was all mine.

Neither Mick Law nor any of his Balloch pals ever bothered me again.

I had a newfound hero status and shrugged off all the congratulations.....

"Ach sure it was nothing....that Mick Law is all talk.....I knew I could beat him"...I lied. Whilst demonstrating the punches I had used to immobilise my victim.

About a month or so later Mick law disappeared from our school. The story was that he ran away from home, went to the Broomielaw in Glasgow and stowed away on an overnight boat for Ireland. After a few weeks of living rough and evading the police he was finally caught, sent back to Balloch and to an approved school for delinquent, uncontrollable boys....I liked to think that he ran away because he couldn't deal with the shame of being defeated in battle by a big, useless, skinny malinky from Brucehill.

As for Marie Bridges ...the day after the fight she sent me a note which was delivered to me on my way to school by one of her friends...

Ah yes.... I thought, this will be a note praising me, her conquering hero, and pledging her undying love until the day we die........I opened the note expectantly and with trembling hands.....

"You're chucked" ....it said.

It was 1966 and I was approaching 15 and still a virgin...... now losing that virginity became a priority.........

My sexual awakening finally came at a house party. There was a severe shortage of entertainment for young teenagers in Dumbarton so we used to go to house parties most weekends. Me and my best friend Mick Casey spent most Saturday afternoons in Casci's Cafe in Church Street, this was our social centre where we could meet other friends, drink hot blackcurrant and chat up girls.

Casci's was a small cafe with about 8 tables and bench seats designed to hold 3 or 4 people comfortably but with so many teenagers in there we usually crowded 8 to 10 on each table. It was a traditional sixties cafe, painted inside in modern style and colours, pink and purple walls and with a Pepsi cola mirror on the wall alongside posters of Cliff Richards, Frank Sinatra and Marylyn Monroe. The big silver espresso coffee machines burbled and steamed constantly and the air was always thick with cigarette smoke. During the week it was the place where housewives out shopping in the town centre, could take a break and meet for a wee blether and a cup of the fashionable new cappuccino coffee, however at the weekends it was the territory of the young teenagers of Dumbarton. In the corner was the "Rockolla" jukebox. For sixpence we could choose three songs from the top twenty. My favourites, being a mod were,

The Four Tops. Reach Out I'll be There....The Small Faces....All Or Nothing and of course The Beatles...Paper Back Writer... When we heard a rumour that a party was happening somewhere that night me and Mick would simply invite ourselves and turn up. Sometimes we would be refused entry and thrown out by the host or a friend of the host when it was discovered that we weren't actually on the guest list, other times we simply said we were friends of Jimmy and he had said it was O.K. for us to come. As Jimmy was a very common boy's name and as most people called friends or strangers Jimmy, everyone knew someone called Jimmy we were on a winner and usually warmly welcomed by the host as any friend of Jimmy was a friend of theirs. We always arrived with a "carry out", a bottle of cheap Eldorado fortified wine we had bought in the Elephant and Castle and put it on the kitchen table then proceeded to drink from the bottles of whisky and beer that the real guests had brought.

So one Saturday in Casci's the rumour was going around that an all-night party was going on that night in a house in Westcliff of a girl we vaguely knew and whose parents would be away for the weekend. This was right up our street as it meant we could walk there and stagger home. Or if we got lucky stay the night.

This party was in a house in Ashton View I can't remember whose house or whose party but as usual we brought our bottle of Eldorado and arrived at the door on the invitation of "Jimmy".

Me and Mick were very popular with the local girls, not because we were outstandingly handsome but even if I say so myself we had charismatic personalities and had "the patter", and in keeping with the 60's teen philosophy we were up for fun and a good time and to hell with the consequences. There was a girl at the party who I knew and had seen her a few times in Casci's and I had been told by all her friends that she fancied me, her name was Liz, she was from Bowling which was a small village near Dumbarton. I also fancied her and knew that it was safe as Bowling, being a small village didn't have a gang who would be after my blood for stealing one of their girls. She was a couple of years older than me at around 17 .I had been told by her friends that she would be "up for it", with me, which meant that she was willing and available for sex. This elusive act which I had read, heard and talked so much about and boasted to all my friends that I had done hundreds of times. Now I was keen to try it with a real, live girl. So the party was off to a great start and me and Mick were drinking, beer and whisky and mingling and dancing with all the girls and generally having a fantastic time. I spotted Liz, she was wearing a fashionable floral pattern mini skirt, long knee-length, black boots, white stockings and a white blouse, her short blond hair was brushed over in the Twiggy style and with pink shiny lipstick and very dark eye shadow and long, false eyelashes which she was now fluttering in my direction, she looked the typical "mod" girl and completely gorgeous. She was dancing with her group of friends and as was the normal procedure I and Mick quickly joined in with them on the floor.

As her friends disappeared one by one into the kitchen or to sit down with a drink we both stayed dancing together along to the music of Diana Ross and the Supremes singing "Baby Love". I was showing off, really impressing her with all the latest dance moves and we were laughing and singing along with Diana. We danced together for a while then we sat on the sofa and talked about music and fashion. We were getting on really well and I was very relaxed possibly due to the effects of the wine, beer and whisky, when suddenly she leaned in and kissed me.

Now I had practised this kissing before down the cliff with my first childhood love Catherine Casey, when we were 8 or 9 years old and we would do "film star kissing, mouths closed and heads turning from side to side. This time it was different, Liz laughed and teased me about my juvenile kissing attempts and showed me how to kiss "properly" with mouths open and tongues exploring the inside of each other's mouths. This new fashionable method of kissing with tongues was a revelation, it felt incredible, I had butterflies in my stomach and my head was spinning. Liz told me it was a new style of kissing called "French Kissing". I remembered at that moment my French teacher Claudia Deauville who appeared regularly in my many wet dreams and fantasies and thought well if this is good enough for the French then it must be good enough for this wee inexperienced Brucehill boy. I was getting aroused and shifting around trying to make space in my tight new Levi jeans which I had bought especially for the party in Edwards menswear shop in the High Street that day, then rubbed them with a cloth soaked in bleach to give them the fashionable "bleached" look which we all loved... I suddenly felt her hand touching the outside of my growing bulge...wow! This was sensational this was the first hand apart from mine and a pervert Irish priest in Ireland which had touched my erect willy. She took my trembling hand and put it up inside her blouse and on top of her padded bra which to my delight contained a real breast inside. I had never felt a real breast before, I had seen them in photos which we passed around in school, and in magazines and often fantasised about how these objects of desire would feel in real life and this was even better than I had dreamt. It was firm and as I clumsily moved my fingers inside her bra they made contact with a hard nipple. She made a soft moaning noise and pulled me closer and all this time our mouths were still locked in the same kiss we had started half an hour before.

Without a word she took my hand, stood up and led me upstairs to one of the bedrooms where another couple were rolling around on top of the bed my head was reeling both with the effects of the alcohol and the situation. As the bed was occupied we lay on the only available space next to the bed on the floor on top of all the guest's jackets and coats which the other couple, in their moments of ecstasy had thrown on the floor, and continued with this fantastic new way of kissing. She lifted her mini skirt up to her waist and put my hand on her thigh. This was incredible, I had my hand on the inside top of her thigh, she was wearing stockings and now I was touching the "promised land" the area of bare flesh between her stocking top and her knickers. I had absolutely no idea what I was supposed to do so just wiggled my fingers around a bit like when I played my guitar and with her moaning and squirming I guessed I must have been doing something right.

She undone my Levis and yanked them down, uncovering my bare spotty arse and all of this without a single word and with our lips permanently locked together, drowning in saliva and with tongues exploring the inside of each other's mouths.

She pulled me over on top of her and I lay between her open legs, there followed a lot of urgent fiddling and fumbling on my part until she gave a helping hand by manoeuvring me into a position where I could penetrate her front bum and I was away...whooohoooo... three or four thrusts later it was all over...Geroooniiiimooo.. I was ecstatic, there was no foreplay and I never gave a thought as to whether she was getting any pleasure or not.

We lay for a few minutes with heavy sighs on the pile of coats, then got up and straightened out our clothes. There was no whispered pillow talk or promises of undying love and marriage. She stood up, fixed her hair and rearranged her clothes and went to the toilet....I could hear music coming from the party downstairs...it was the Beach Boys singing Good Vibrations......

We staggered back down to join the party, I caught a glimpse of Mick on the sofa with a girl, he just looked at me and winked and put up his thumb...I returned the gesture and we both smiled and nodded.

Me and Liz danced to Diana Ross and the Supremes. You Can't Hurry Love......and talked and kissed and danced and drank some more then at the end of the party she left with her friends.........I thought....Oh Shit!!!...I forgot to ask her if she was a catholic.....

I saw her a couple of times after the party in Casci's on a Saturday afternoon with her group of friends and we just exchanged hellos and smiles but I have never forgotten her or that historic night...whenever I hear those songs I remember that momentous occasion.

This wasn't the scenario for losing my virginity which I had imagined there were no fireworks exploding in the sky...no choir of heavenly angels singing the hallelujah chorus....Just The Who singing My Generation. This front bum experience wasn't what I had envisaged in my fantasies, however, I had learnt new techniques and I was determined to keep practicing until I got it right.

I was eternally grateful to Liz.....I'm sure that she must have realized that I was a virgin and a complete amateur, despite my confident exterior but what she didn't know was that I was really, secretly, very insecure and even doubted at times my sexuality. My body had betrayed me when a paedophile catholic priest sexually abused me in Ireland at a boy's guild summer camp two years earlier when life stole my innocence and since that time I had been experiencing some psychological problems relating to my sexuality. I was convinced I must be homosexual because my body had, on that occasion reacted to sexual stimulation by a man and although I knew I preferred and fancied girls and could easily get aroused by looking at pictures of naked women, I was nevertheless extremely confused.

Because of that night and with Liz's help I was free from doubt and knew for sure that all my fears and worries were unfounded...I was definitely heterosexual and very, very happy. Now with this new found confidence and experience I was keen to teach every teenage girl in Dumbarton this new, exciting French kissing and front bum activity.

Contraception was never used by boys in those days and was practically unheard of and not freely available. It was always assumed that as good catholic boys we wouldn't be having sex until we were married and then of course only when we wanted to make babies and so no family planning education was necessary.

Our idea of "safe sex" was never to tell a girl your address.

For teenage girls the new contraceptive pill was available, however, for catholic girls it was impossible to get permission from their strict parents to get it on prescription as the Catholic Church forbade any form of contraception. Many teenagers were ignorant of the methods and so were unaware of birth control options. The extent of our sex education was when the priest visited our school and explained whilst blushing profusely and shuffling his feet nervously, that we should never touch our erect penis.

But here we were in the swinging sixties the decade of Sex, Drugs and Rock n Roll of Free Love, Hippies and Flower Power. The sexual revolution was well under way and we were the generation who invented it. Whenever I had sex in my teenage years I never used a condom and intended every time to use the withdrawal method, as recommended by the Catholic Church, otherwise known to me and all my friends by the euphemism of "Jumping off at Dalreoch."

Which referred to the three train stations in Dumbarton.........

"Hey Big Yin did ye score last night?"

"Aye I lumbered a wee Glasgow hairy and shagged her in the car."

"Aye and did ye jump aff at Dalreoch or stay on to Dumbarton Central."

"Well, I tried to get aff at Dalreoch but the train was going at full speed and couldn't get aff at The Central either....I stayed on to Dumbarton East."

I think I was lucky that none of my conquests got pregnant or that I didn't catch or spread any sexually transmitted diseases........that I know of.....

I blame Ellen Gren for showing me her front bum when I was a wee innocent impressionable 7 year old boy.........

Teen Years and Leaving Home.

1966...

The Vietnam War was in full swing with The U.S.A sending even more fresh faced, young teenagers to face death in a controversial, hopeless war.

The British Government announced the death of shillings and pennies and from 1971 British currency would be decimal.

The British Labour Party led by Harold Wilson won the general election.

The moors murderers Ian Brady and Myra Hindley were both sentenced to life imprisonment for the murders of children in Yorkshire.

In New York the foundations were laid for what would be two of the highest skyscrapers in the city...named The Twin Towers.

The Beatles were at the top of the charts with "We can work it out" with the Rolling Stones right behind with "Paint it black"

Oh.....and England won the world cup...in case you hadn't heard, beating Germany in the final 4-2.........

....and I left St Patrick's High School.....

I was told by most of my teachers that I had O level, A level and even university potential.

I wanted to be a commercial artist, so needed O and A levels in art, English and science.

These were my favourite subjects and I was seriously considering staying on and taking the exams to continue in further education and go to university and a future career in art.

However, fate took control of my destiny.

I received the offer of an apprenticeship as a painter and decorator with a family firm in Helensburgh, H Waddell and son, who offered me a 4 year apprenticeship with one day a week at Clydebank technical college to train for a City & Guilds diploma as a sign writer and two evenings a week at the Glasgow school of art to study Illustration and Calligraphy.

This was right up my street, a job with albeit low wages and the opportunity to progress my career in an artistic way. The offer was just too tempting and so after careful consideration, I accepted the job.

So in December 1966 I left St Patrick's High. I walked out of the gates for the last time with mixed feelings.

Thanks to my 11 years of education, both academic and social. And because of or despite the harsh discipline I felt fully competent and able to face the big wide world as an adult.

I can't say that I loved school, neither did hate it.But I survived it...I loved learning, and had it not been for the strict discipline and some cruel, sadistic teachers I am sure I would have enjoyed it even more. The discipline was at times hard to accept, but the lessons and life skills, both academic and social, I learned have served me well throughout my life.

Thank you St Pats both wee and big...you took a wee scruffy, shy boy from Dumbarton and by fair means or foul, turned him into the confident, successful, well rounded human being that he is today.

H Waddell and son was a small family business which had been started by the grandfather of the current manager Lesley Waddell and carried out high class decoration of the rich house owners in Helensburgh and surrounding towns of Cardross, Rhu and Garelochhead.

There were three tradesmen, Jimmy McGhee, Arthur Cooper and Kurt Fleischer

I was assigned as apprentice to Jimmy McGhee, whose previous apprentice, I was told, had left and set up his own decorating business in the town.

I knew from the first day that I wasn't going to get on too well with Jimmy McGhee. He was a very stern, strict and demanding tradesman and treated me as his personal slave. I knew that I had a lot to learn about the trade and that, although I was keen and a fast learner I had difficulty in meeting his exacting demands from day one.

I had been used to strict discipline in school and thought that working life would be different, but how wrong I was. Jimmy McGhee was my slave master and he would bark orders at me and criticize everything I did from 8.00 am to 4.30 when my working day finished.

My only respite came every Wednesday when I went to Clydebank Technical College for my day in class learning the theoretical aspect of painting and decorating. And two evenings a week I was attending the Glasgow School of Art in Renfrew Street. Jimmy was dead against this form of training, he believed that apprentices needed to learn from a tradesman by doing all the dirty, preparation jobs which tradesmen were above and that any form of college education was a pointless waste of time. I had to sandpaper walls until my fingers bled, mix Polyfilla for him to apply, and god help me if the consistency of the mixture was too thick or thin. I had to wash floors, clean the old varnish off doors using neat ammonia and boiling water which burned my skin and made my eyes sting and water so much that I couldn't see anything., I wouldn't be allowed to even touch a paint brush apart from cleaning them, until my second year.

The other two tradesmen had their respective apprentices both of whom were in their second year and were painting and hanging wallpaper too. When we all worked together on big, posh houses above Helensburgh I was the one who had to make the tea and sweep the floors and take orders from all the others.

This is not what I expected and I became very disillusioned.

I came home from work every day and complained to my mum about my treatment and my dissappointment.My Mum said that I should stick at it as it would get better. I took her advice and put up with Jimmy McGhee using me as slave labour.

I began evening classes at the Glasgow School of Art and would go up to Glasgow twice a week on my scooter for Calligraphy and Illustration classes. I loved this, it gave me the opportunity to learn a new artistic skill which I hoped in the future would give me the qualifications and skills I would need to throw off my chains of slavery and improve my prospects of becoming an Illustrator or Signwriter.

In the second year of my apprenticeship things improved slightly and I was now allowed to use a paintbrush albeit only for undercoating or painting the dirty jobs which Jimmy felt were too menial for him to do. In my class at Clydebank Tech was another boy the same age as me from Dumbarton, his name was Bobby Meldrum. Bobby worked as a painter for Dumbarton Town Council and was always telling me about how fantastic it was and how much fun he had with him and his workmates always playing jokes on each other and how relaxed his tradesmen were. It was the extreme opposite from my situation and realizing that my job was not what I expected I decided to investigate the possibilities of finding a job like his.

It was January and snowing and so one day when I couldn't go to Clydebank on my scooter I took the opportunity to be proactive and went down to the Dumbarton Town Council works department which was behind the Central Station. I just walked in and asked for the manager who Bobby had told me was a man named John Donnelly.

John was a friendly, helpful man and I explained my situation and how I was training to be a sign writer and attending classes at Glasgow School of Art.John knew my dad as at that time he was driving the bin lorries and he said he would speak to his bosses and see what he could do. A couple of days later my dad told me that John Donnelly had called him into the office and told him that I should go back and see him as he had some news for me.The next morning I got my mum to go out to the phone box and phone Lesley Waddell and say I was ill and couldn't come to work, and went straight down to the works department to speak to John.

John Donnelly told me that their signwriter,Jimmy Johnston was going to retire the following year and that his bosses had given him the go ahead to take on an apprentice who could take over the signwriting duties when Jimmy retired, so would I like to take up the position.

He didn't need to ask me twice. I went to Helensburgh the next day and gave Lesley Waddell a week's notice. The old bastard Jimmy McGhee said that he was quite happy because I was useless and would never be a high class painter and decorator like him.

Working at Dumbarton Town Council was everything Bobby Meldrum had told me it would be. There was a group of about 12 qualified painters and three apprentices the signwriting was mainly road signs and street signs and when there was no signwriting we would just go out to the other painting jobs and help out. We had our own little minivan which I was allowed to drive and as long as I was working could use it to nip home for lunch or the odd cup of tea. If we were out on jobs and we had finished the signs we could just go back to the yard or sneak off home. It was fantastic and completely opposite from my two years of slavery in Helensburgh.

The group of painters were all friends and accepted me as one of them. We had nights out together and would often go to the pub after work and have a few beers together.

An added bonus of being a painter was that now I was having neighbours knocking on the door asking if I could paint their houses, so some evenings and weekends I spent decorating houses and of course earning extra money which helped to finance running my car and paying Art School fees which up until then my parents had to subsidise, buying all the latest trendy clothes and going on holidays and going out dancing and drinking on Saturday nights.

The highlight of my time at Dumbarton Council was when the painters were re-decorating Overtoun House. It was going to be used as a children's nursery and the council wanted to brighten it up with bright colours and paintings of cartoon characters on the walls. So I had the job to paint cartoon murals on all the walls. I spent a few months there painting, Mickey Mouse, Donald Duck, and scenes from all the Disney films including the sleeping Beauty, Snow White and the seven Dwarfs on the walls of The Angel Room the same room where I had been born 18 years before.

My best friend was Mick Casey. I had known Mick since we lived next to each other in Castlehill when we were 5 years old, we went through school together. Mick was much like me, full of fun, adventurous and loved the girlies.We had some fantastic adventures and together with Jim Foley and Tom (Sneb) Robinson we were typical teenagers. Our big advantage was that I had a car and so we could travel to Glasgow or Edinburgh on a Saturday night in search of new talent. Or as Mick put it "fresh meat".

Sunday nights was Duck Bay Marina where all the local girls needed a lift home.

Mick had the gift of the gab. I was shy and felt awkward about approaching girls. Not mick.

Most boys used the recognised clichéd chat-up lines...

Never seen you here before ...Do you come here often? Where have you been all my life? What is a beautiful girl like you doing in a place like this? etc.

Not for Mick and me these old, worn out chat-ups.

If we saw two girls we liked the look of, Mick would simply saunter up to them......

"Why are you two girls staring at us?"

"What? Staring at you two eedjits...gie's a break son were no desperate."

"Well me and my friend Joe here have been watching you two and you keep on staring at us."

"Aye because yer both pot ugly that's why."

"Ok ...Ok calm down...sorry I made a mistake, we thought you fancied us."

After 10 minute we would pass the same two girls again…..

"See you're both staring at us again …so which one of us do you fancy?"

Mick would say flashing his cheeky smile….

"Can we dance with you and talk about it?"

So we would have a dance with them all the time winning them over with our cheeky, couldn't care less attitude…..and at the end he would ask them if they wanted to buy us a drink .

"Whit??...You two cheeky bastards really fancy your chances eh...it's supposed to be the boy who buys the girl drinks."

"Aye but were different and if you want us to give you a lift home tonight you need to buy us a drink first."

This tactic worked most of the time and amazingly 9 out of 10 girls took us to the bar, opened their purses and bought us drinks.

Many weekends just for a change of scenery we would drive to Edinburgh.

Edinburgh had a fantastic night life and we would begin the night in Rose Street.

Rose Street is a narrow cobbled street which runs parallel to Princes Street and is full of pubs.

Edinburgh's attraction for us was the huge amount of students particularly nurses who were training in the Western General Hospital and living in the city centre and who all began their night out in Rose Street. These student nurses were always having parties and so we would chat them up and discover where the parties were and solicit an invitation. If we couldn't get invited we would simply turn up later at the address when everyone was drunk and walk in the open front door, or wait until two girls arrived at the door and talk them into pretending we were with them. Once inside we usually found a couple of available girls or if not just enjoyed the party and the free booze provided by the host or the genuine guests.

These weekends made a welcome change from the scene in Dumbarton and we found ourselves becoming very popular with the Edinburgh students and often being officially invited to nurse's parties.

1968…

Martin Luther King…Had a Dream…Then he was assassinated by James Earl Ray.

Harold Wilson was the Labour Prime Minister and we were all "Backing Britain."

The notorious gang leaders "The Kray twins were arrested.

The Beatles film "Yellow submarine" had its debut in London.

The controversial musical "Hair" opened in London with demonstrators protesting in Leicester Square about the gratuitous nudity content.

And my big sister left home.

Marie Therese had met an English boy when she was on holiday at Butlin's.His name was Dave Briglin and she fell in love. When the holiday was over she came back home and just cried most of the time and she missed Dave very much, she went to visit him in Hull and he came and stayed with us in Brucehill some weekends. All the family fully approved of Dave despite his two major faults. He was English *AND* a protestant. He was forced to join in the singing at our many family parties, despite this he asked Marie Therese to marry him so my sister moved to Hull to live with Dave's family until they got married the following year.

My sister leaving home affected me more than I had thought.

At first the thought of my life without my tormentor would be, in my opinion more peaceful and quiet. However, in reality I missed my best friend and worst enemy more than I had imagined.

Throughout our childhood Marie Therese was a prominent figure in my life. When we were children she teased me relentlessly and at times I could happily have strangled her ,buried her alive in a shallow grave and spent the rest of my life in prison without a second thought, but in my teenage years she was my mentor, best friend, my confidante and my ally against our parents strict household rules.

We shared our secrets and confided in each other about girlfriend/boyfriend problems.

She used me as her adviser when she wanted to go to Glasgow clothes shopping and needed advice she often took me, asked my advice then completely ignored it and chose exactly what she wanted no matter what I said. Once she even tricked me into going with her on a first date because she was shy.

She had met Ronnie Leahy, a boy who played keyboards in a group called The Pathfinders and they arranged to meet in Glasgow outside Queen Street station. She kept this information secret until we arrived at the station, then continued with the trickery by passing the time when we were waiting for him to show up by pointing to every ugly, fat boy who walked in our direction and telling me that this was him coming now. I am sure that Ronnie was as pleased as me to discover that his new hot date had dragged along her spotty, annoying little brother on their first date. She had to buy me pokey hats for a month as bribes when Palombo's ice cream van appeared in Brucehill to compensate and to stop me telling our Parents.

Dumbarton High Street on a Saturday afternoon was teenager's hunting ground, the girls would parade around in groups on one side of the street and the boys on the other, and there was always a constant stream of boys and girls crossing the road to ask if someone would go out with one of their mates. When my sister wanted to go down to Dumbarton High street on a Saturday afternoon "Talent Spotting" she would order me to come with her as she didn't want to go on her own…. promising to buy me a bag of broken biscuits from Woolworths or a bag of toffee from Minnie Steele's in Church Street……or threatening to divulge to our parents that I had been seen with a wee proddy lassie.

"Mammy….. Tell Joe he has to come to town with me."

"Joe ...go down the High Street with your sister."

"But mum...I don't want to go to town."

"JOE...Go with Marie Therese and don't argue."

So I had to go with her in case she saw a boy she fancied then she could send me to ask him to go out with her.

The following week when she had friends to go with and I wanted to go with her it was a different story.....

"Mammy tell Joe that he can't come to town with me and to stop following me around and showing me up."

"Joe you stay here and leave your sister alone...she doesn't want her wee brother following her around in the High Street."

"But mammy last week "........

"JOE...Do as yer told and don't argue."

So Marie Therese left home to live in Hull and with only me and my mum and dad the house seemed very empty. Although I was happy for her that she had finally found someone she loved and was going to get married and settle down with I really missed her and her company and her moral support at home.

My Mum and Dad argued a lot and I was always used as the go-between when after an argument they didn't speak to each other for days or sometimes weeks.

"Joe...go and tell yer dad his dinners on the table."

Although my dad would be sitting on his chair by the fire reading a book and the table was at arm's length.

"Dad my mum says yer dinner's on the table."

"Aye right son...tell her I'll be there as soon as I finish this chapter."

"Mum. He says he'll be five minutes."

"Tell him if he's no at this table in one minute then his dinner will be in the bin."

"Dad...mum says "........

"Aye right son I heard her".......

Now with only three of us at home my mum decided it was time to move to a smaller house with only two bedrooms.

So off she went to the council offices to work her magic and we moved to Glencairn Road.

Number 44 was our new house, below us was Johnny and Angie McGee and next door Eddie Wolfries.

Johnny and Angie were a lovely couple. They never had any children and I think through some psychological problems Johnny turned to drink. At times he managed to keep it under control but then relapsed and hit the bottle again. We could hear poor frustrated Angie shouting at him late at night when he staggered in drunk yet again.

Now with only my Aunt Annie left at home my grannie Gow had also moved out of her huge house in Caledonia Terrace and was now living in Brucehill Road at number 4, opposite my Auntie Marie now living at no 26, and who had married a lovely man from Govan called Tommy Bell who she had met on at the Flamingo ballroom in Paisley Road in Glasgow on a night out dancing with my sister and all their friends.

It was the end of an era of our lives in Caledonia Terrace and the start of a new one.

I was enjoying my job and had a fantastic social life, with money in my pocket and my own car, life was good.

1970

The Isle of White music festival attracted 500,000 people who danced to the music of Jimmy Hendrix, The Doors and The Who...whilst in a field somewhere near a small, remote, village by the name of Glastonbury in Somerset, a local farmer named Michael Eaves opened the gates of one of his fields so that 200 hippies, returning from the summer solstice at Stonehenge could hold a free music festival and smoke marijuana.

The commonwealth games were held in Edinburgh.

The top selling cars were the Ford Escort, Hillman Avenger and Vauxhall Viva.If you wanted one it would cost £659 pounds then fill the tank with petrol from Buchanan's garage at Dalreoch for 34p a gallon.

The general election saw the departure of the Labour Prime Minister Harold Wilson and the dawn of a new conservative government headed by Ted Heath.

In the summer of 1970 ,me ,Mick Casey, Jim Foley and Sneb Robinson went on holiday together to Butlin's Holiday camp in Filey in Yorkshire .We were 18,we had survived the Swinging Sixties and were now ready for the Sexy Seventies. We were on the loose from our parents and took full advantage of being young, free and single.

We had such a fantastic time, made some great friends and met some beautiful girls so we decided that as we had enjoyed ourselves so much the we should come back the following year but instead of on holiday, we could get summer jobs.

The idea grew with me and Mick getting excited and enthusiastic about the prospect of spending the following summer working at Butlin's, however, Jim was an apprentice electrician in John Browns shipyard in Clydebank and couldn't take 3 months off, Sneb had a regular girlfriend Vera and he decided that he couldn't take a sabbatical either, So with Mick working as a van boy in Caulfield's fruit shop and me with Dumbarton County Council, we decided that our jobs were not as important as having an adventure working at Butlin's.

My parents were dead against the idea as they continually reminded me that I had a job for life with the council and was continuing with my degree course at the Glasgow School of Art. However, my opinion was that life was too short and as I was only going to be young once I could always crawl back to the council and beg for my job back, and my Art School course finished in June and started again in September, so as far as I was concerned I was going despite my mum's protestations. I needed an adventure and as I was now 18, and considered an adult and responsible for my own decisions I told them that I was going and suffered the arguments followed by the silent treatment from my mum for weeks before my grannie convinced her to let me make my own mistakes in life as, in her opinion, I would learn more from them.

We applied for jobs in January leaving the location blank so that we would go to any centre which needed staff. And had our acceptance letters in April. We could start in May in Butlin's in Bognor Regis. We had never heard of Bognor Regis, it was on the south coast of England in Sussex. I was accepted as a driver and Mick as a cellarman.My job was to drive a minibus collecting new staff from railway stations and bus stations and transporting them to the camp before the holiday makers arrived and during the season, any driving duties which included driving the tourist train around the camp, and Mick's was to keep the bars and restaurants cellars full of beer and alcohol for the holidaymakers.

So in the middle of May 1971 we left Dumbarton and headed for Sussex.Butlin's paid our travel expenses and we set off for Glasgow Central to travel to London, Waterloo station then another train to Bognor Regis.

We were excited about our big adventure and arrived at the camp reception and were allocated our chalets. We soon made friends with other staff who were also starting in May to prepare for the camp opening in June for the holiday season.

The staff chalets were the same as the holiday chalets and we shared J110.The wages were very low, about £7 a week, however, we had all our meals and accommodation provided and as our friends worked in restaurants and bars we were never short of extra free food and drink.

There was a permanent party atmosphere and we had welcome parties in our chalets for all the new staff arriving. My job as a mini bus driver meant that I was the first person the new staff met when they arrived at the station and also meant that I was the talent scout looking out for girls who I fancied and then telling Mick when I came back that we had dates for that night.

Life was just one huge party and we loved every minute of it.

Butlin's was originally the invention of Sir Billy Butlin who after the war realized that British people needed somewhere cheap they could go on holiday with their families which provided non-stop entertainment and cheap accommodation with the help of Redcoats who were the camp entertainers to ensure that they always were being entertained and taking the children off the parents hands with their children's clubs so that the parents could be free to have a drink and enjoy themselves safe in the knowledge that their kids were being well looked after. It was an enormous success and other camps soon opened all over the U.K.

I was now quite good at playing guitar and so with some other staff who could play we formed a group and were allowed to play in the bars and lounges of the camp and get paid with beer which suited us perfectly.

We could also join in with the holidaymakers in the bars and discos in our free time and would meet girls who were on holiday and persuade them to take us out for drinks as we were only poor Butlin's staff. Our dreams were coming true and we never regretted for one minute abandoning our jobs in Dumbarton and embracing this adventure.

We returned to Dumbarton at the end of the season in September. Mick went back to his job in Caulfield's but I was very unsettled and needed more.

After such a wonderful experience working at Butlin's the prospect of settling back down to my routine job in the council didn't appeal to me at all. I needed more adventure. I was restless.

I explained to my parents that I couldn't go back to a dead end job and wanted to leave home and be independent. They of course disapproved and tried to make me change my mind. However, after many huge arguments I managed to convince them that I was now an adult and responsible for my own destiny and would be going to visit my sister in Hull and at the same time look for a job and a flat.

So that is exactly what I did. Marie Therese and Dave were my saviours and offered to put me up until I found a job and accommodation so in January 1972 I left Dumbarton, found a new exciting job as a signwriter and painter with an exhibition company in Hull and shared a house with some crazy hippies from Newcastle and started a new life and adventure in England.

Dumbarton...The town of my birth, my childhood and my teenage years is and always will be my home and will always have a special place in my heart

The town, it's people, it's worthies like Big Freddy Waymark......

"You got nice hair...what time on you watch?"

Whitey O'Neil, staggering, drunkenly in the middle of the High Street and directing the buses around him.

Big Cool Gallagher standing in the triangle in Caledonia Terrace blind drunk on a Friday night challenging everybody to come out onto the triangle and fight him until his tiny, old mother came out, reached up, grabbed him by the scruff of the neck and marched him back into the house whist raining blows to the side of his head.

Wee Jackie Mitchell my dad's workmate and wingman with his silly jokes.....

"Hey Joe what d'ye call a man with size 12 shoes and no dug?......Big shoey dugless."

Wee Dick Ponsonby and the town drunks drinking Eldorado and Vordo "doon the quay". The shows in the common every August always bringing the rain.

Minnie Steel's legendary, tablet and toffee. Mary Baker's, Casci's Cafe, Tony Biaggi's chip shop, and the busy shops in the high street before the council ruined it with their tragic planning decisions. The pubs, The Burgh Hall……. These are the people and things that gave Dumbarton its heartbeat. Sadly all gone in times past.

Dumbartonians are a unique dying breed of people.

When I lived in Dumbarton everyone knew everyone and the town was like one big, happy family. You couldn't just nip down the High Street for a few massages, you were bound to be stopped for a wee blether a dozen times by neighbours or friends who had to share with you the latest gossip about that wee wifie Mrs So an So's son getting arrested by the polis or that wee grannie So and So passing away suddenly, or the ultimate scandal that Wee Lassie Mctavish getting pregnant and her only just left school and getting a good job in Ballantine's Distillery .(the word "pregnant" always being whispered in a low voice) The spirit of kindness and friendliness was tangable.The sarcastic sense of humour relentless.

When Celtic and Rangers were playing the town was divided with workmates and neighbours turning into sworn enemies for 90 minutes until later in the pubs hands were shaken and pints of heavy and wee chasers were shared then staggering down the High Street, arms around shoulders singing Flower of Scotland together.

For such a small town Dumbarton has a huge heart. I have met Sons and Daughters of The Rock in many strange corners and far flung lands. Once in New York in an Irish bar full of New Yorkers on New Year's Eve the barman, recognising my accent asked which part of Scaaaatlaaand I came from. It turned out his uncle had worked in Denny's with my dad in the early sixties before emigrating to the U.S.A. He bought me a few whiskies and we sang Auld Lang Syne together at the bells along with all the other customers.

On a ferry between two remote Islands in Indonesia I noticed a young man sitting opposite had exactly the same tattoo as me, A Celtic cross, with the motto, in Latin, "Fortis Et Fidus".Unable to contain my curiosity I had to ask him.

He smiled and explained that he was an Australian from Perth but his father was Scottish.

And his name was John McLaughlin, from a small town which I had probably never heard of called Dumbarton and that the motto meant "brave and faithful" which was the family motto of the Clan McLaughlin.

He nearly fell overboard when I showed him my tattoo with the exact same motto and told him that I was also a "Son of the Rock" and had gone to St Patrick's High School with his dad.

On a long flight to Saint Lucia I found myself sitting next to a businessman who was travelling to a meeting with the government in Castries. He was English but his ex-wife was from Dumbarton and they had lived Merkins Avenue in Bellsmyre when they were married. We spent the flight reminiscing about Scotland in general and Dumbarton in particular.

In a small local bar in a back street in Shanghai the barman asked me in his bad English…

"Whell you flom?..You Engreesh?"

"No…I come from Scotland…do you know where that is?"

"No..No.. I doe no whel Scotrand is…..Is it in Engerand?"

I was just about to launch into a geography lesson when I spotted a bottle of Ballantine's Whisky on the shelf.

I pointed to it and said..

"Pass me that bottle and I'll explain."

I pointed to the label which says "Brewed in Dumbarton"

"This is my town…I said…puffing out my chest with pride."

"Ahhh Barrantine…you flom Barrantine."

"No…No…Oh never mind just pour me a large one."

Ballantine's whisky almost as famous a Dumbarton icon as the castle itself, is sold in almost every country in the world and still says on its label" ***Brewed in Dumbarton, Scotland*** " although the red brick distillery building stopped brewing whisky many years ago and only partly remains and still stands as a silent, ghostly reminder of the past.

Here in Spain where I now live there are many Scots who, like me have swapped the cold Scottish weather for a much healthier, warmer climate not to mention the cheap alcohol and healthy diet. I know people here from Duntocher, Balloch, Clydebank and Glasgow. Of course I consider it my crusade now in my life as an English teacher to educate my students about Scotland and its rich Celtic culture as many believe that it is part of England, a mistake which I never fail to correct on many occasions. Many Spanish people think that if someone speaks English then they must be from England, which I explain is an insult to any patriotic, true blooded Scotsman.

My town of birth Dumbarton, although changed dramatically has the most important component still unbreakably intact….its proud people.

Dumbarton made me the person I am today. All my childhood experiences good and bad formed my character and the structure of my life. I miss the old Dumbarton and will always call it home.

On my last nostalgic visit with the memories swirling around my head like a whirlwind I realized how lucky I am…. Lucky to have lived in an unrepeatable time and place in history… Lucky to have been born into such a wonderful family….Lucky and proud to have been "Made in Dumbarton" and of being a genuine Son of the Rock…….Lucky and eternally grateful for my Dumbarton Childhood.

THE END

Dictionary of Scottish Dialect

Aye-Yes

Ach-Oh

Awa-Away

An-And

A'-All

Aff-Off

Backside-Bottom

Bahookie-Bottom

Couldnae-Couldn't

C'mere-Come here

Chib-weapon (knife or sharpened steel comb)

Doon-Down

Durty-Dirty

Dis-Does

Disnae-Doesn't

Dyke-Wall

Doo-Pigeon

Eedjit...Idiot

Fae-From

Fur-For

Gie-Give

Gied-Gave

Hoose-House

Heilan-Highland

Hame-Home

Hen-Daughter

Huv-Have

Huvnae-Haven't

Intae-Into

Jist-Just

Lumber-take a girl/boy home.

Maw-Mum

Mammy-Mummy

Noo-Now

Oot-Out

Skinny-thin

Skinny malinky Long Legs-Tall,thin with long legs.

Wid-Would

Widnae-Wouldn't

Whit-What

Wee-Small

Winchin-Serious relationship

Ye-You

Yer-Your

Printed in Great Britain
by Amazon